A TIME FOR LIVING

by Jill Briscoe

An *ideals* Publication

ACKNOWLEDGMENTS

Unless otherwise identified, all Scripture quotations are from the King James Version of the Bible.

Verses marked Living Bible are taken from The Living Bible, copyright 1971 by Tyndale House Publishers, Wheaton, Ill. Used by permission. Verse marked RSV from the Revised Standard Version Bible, copyrighted 1946, 1952, © 1971, 1973. GENESIS, copyrighted by and used with permission of Brian Morris. Our sincere thanks to the following author whose address we were unable to locate: Beatrice Cleland for INDWELT.

ISBN 0-89542-078-3 595

Copyright © MCMLXXX by Jill Briscoe

Published by Ideals Publishing Corporation
11315 Watertown Plank Road
Milwaukee, Wisconsin 53226

Contents

What Shall I Do with Jesus
  Who Is Called Christ? 5

Happiness Is 11

Now Barabbas Was a Robber 19

When the Right Feeling Is Wrong 25

Sir, We Remember 35

Who Will Roll Away the Stone? 45

Failure Isn't Final 53

The Fragrant Act of Love 59

Start Where You Are 67

The Things Concerning Himself 75

"To every thing there is a season, and a time to every purpose under the heaven. . . . whatsoever God doeth, it shall be for ever" *(Eccl. 3:1, 14a).*

"Pilate saith unto him, What shall I do then with Jesus which is called Christ? They all say unto him, Let him be crucified" (Matt. 27:22).

What Shall I Do with Jesus Who Is Called Christ?

PILATE: What shall I do with Jesus who is called Christ?

Face to face with the God who made him, Pilate couldn't shake His hand because God's hands were tied; he couldn't say how glad he was to see Him, because he wasn't. He wasn't expecting Him—not here, not now. What on earth was the God of Heaven doing inciting a riot in Jerusalem anyway? Pilate couldn't offer Him a seat because there was only one seat: his judgment throne. This was his province and he was the governor. So just what was it about this exhausted, haggard prisoner that made Pilate want to stand up, change places, and plead for his own life? Somehow he knew he ought to thank Him for the gift of life itself, but turmoil had paralyzed his mind. He was being forced to decide to put the Giver of Life to death.

PILATE: What shall I do with Jesus who is called Christ?

What will you do with Jesus who is called Christ this Eastertime? Face to face with the God who made you, you cannot shake His hand because His hands are tied by you: tied to keep them off your life, to stop them from interfering, to give your spirit liberty to sin. You cannot say how glad you are to see Him because you're not—not here, not now. You, too, can do without the God of Heaven inciting a riot in your capital city, disturbing your peace, challenging the religion that is devoid of the reality in your life. You will not offer Him a seat. There is only one, and it is your throne. You have become His judge, His governor; this is your province. But if you would take only one look into the haggard face of your prisoner, you, like Pilate, would feel compelled to change places and plead for your life. What will you do with Jesus who is called Christ?

PILATE: What shall I do with Jesus who is called Christ?

PILATE'S WIFE: Ignore Him! Have nothing to do with that just man. I fell asleep and dreamed a dream, a terrible fantasy, and how glad I was to wake and find Him gone! Ignore Him and He will go away. Pretend it is only a dream, that He doesn't really exist at all; refuse a confrontation.

PILATE: How can I? I, too, have been so glad to wake from Christ-filled dreams to my realities . . . my solid, harsh, pragmatic world. But now the dream is real; He will not go away. What shall I do with Jesus who is called Christ?

I'll send Him to Herod! He needs Jesus so much more than I do! That old fox could do with a bit of religion to straighten him up! If I send Him to Herod it gets me off the hook; it gives me time.

Do you send Him to Herod? Do you sit in church, confronted by the preaching of God's Word that pierces your soul and demands a response, and look around as Pilate did for someone worse than you, whose need you think is greater than your own? You are sending Him to Herod. But you'll find He'll be back, mocked and scorned and spat upon by those who made their sport at His expense; and still He'll stand and pray that you will release His life, untie His hands and let Him touch you.

PILATE: What shall I do with Jesus who is called Christ? I find no fault in Him at all. What has He done? Certainly nothing worthy of death! This man was born to be free! My world has need of Him, to help the blind to see, the dumb to speak, the lame to walk. And yet He stands my prisoner, allowing me the power of choice to release or crucify. It isn't fair! I don't want to kill Him—I wish Him only kindness, fairness. But listen to the crowd! Crescendo noise that frightens me. Screams of hate prevailing against the forgiving silence of God's Son. I wash my hands, and in the washing stain my soul.

Whatever you do with Christ, as Pilate found, God will let you do.

CENTURION: What shall I do with Jesus who is called Christ? I watched His mockery of a trial and then I had to execute His punishment, and for what? We scourged Him first. To strip His back of flesh, to mock Him and make sport, to spit into His face and ridicule His kingly claim, to pluck the beard from off His cheeks and drive the thorny crown upon His brows these are punishment for the vilest deed alone. But then to crucify, and for what? To throw the cross upon His back, to see Him stumble forth, His great strong-muscled arms adjusting to the weight of it, the hate of it, was more than I could take! And when He fell, the black man took the beam and carried it for Him. The whole world seemed to tramp at my feet. And Simon of Cyrene, at first outraged, became the willing helper to this man, who every now and then would look at him as if to say, "The cross is yours—not mine, but all I ask of you is that you carry it for me. When the time arrives you may give it up, and I will die on it for you." The hill, at last!

The two thieves, whipped and whimpering, began to dig their graves. Resisting the ridiculous, unsoldierly impulse to dig His hole for Him, I handed Him the spade; and as He dug, so strong and deep, I had the strangest knowledge that this man was telling me He wouldn't be using it. Somehow I knew He understood the pity in my heart and the things I *had* to do; I knew also it would be all right. The hammer weighed a ton. The nails seemed to be chained into the ground. Dragging my eyes from Him as my soldiers laid Him, bare, upon the cross, I gave my orders as if my voice belonged to someone else. Or did I just wish that it belonged to someone else?

CENTURION: Stretch Him out upon the cross!
You'll need to keep Him from struggling!
Get His arms!
Pass the nails and hammer!
Hit it hard!
Drive them into the center of His palms!

SOLDIER: That's strange,
He doesn't try to struggle.
Maybe He's exhausted.

CENTURION: Now His feet!
This'll sound good.
We don't want all you rulers disappointed.
Raise the cross and drop it in!

SOLDIER: Ah, grotesque sight,
All major bones disjointed!
God bless this fellow.

CENTURION: No howls of pain?
No craving calls for mercy?
I've killed before;
What's wrong with me?
I've watched the sun
A naked body burn.
Games of dice may clear my mind.
Move over, man.
Give me a throw.
My turn!

SOLDIER: I have no mind for games

GOLGOTHA

With this man hanging
Between earth and heaven.

CENTURION: Why don't your curses burn the air?
We're hardened soldiers,
We won't blush.
Let go!
The man! He thirsts! The vinegar. . . .

SOLDIER: Crucifixion is so ghastly slow!
The silence of this man
Is louder in my ears
Than the two thieves' screams.

CENTURION: I take your life.
You seem to make a gift of it
To me, your murderer,
Almost as if you *want* to die,

As if it were prearranged I'd meet you here.

SOLDIER: I'm losing my reason.
I can't look away from your eyes.

THIEF: This cross seems shaped to fit my life,
Not yours.
The darkness, too,
Is somehow mine.
You saved my crucifixion. Man,
Truly you are the Son of God divine!

CENTURION: I've killed you, God!
God is no more.
God is dead!
Just when I'd found Him.
You speak!
You send your spirit home,
Not just to heaven.

Oh, let me have a part!
I killed your body, Son of God,
And so released your spirit
For my heart!

NICODEMUS: What shall I do with Jesus who is called Christ? I came by night to ask Him for eternal life. By night I came to take His impaled body from the cross. By night I wrapped Him in fresh linen and by night I laid Him in the garden tomb. I came by night because I am afraid. A believer in mourning, I came to do for Him, the Lord of Heaven, my last service. I am a "by night disciple" because my God is dead!

MAGDALENE: What shall I do with Jesus who is called Christ? I came by day to bury Him. I fear no man when I have known the company of demons. I only fear existence without Jesus, and my day is night, my world a world of tears. I watched Him on the cross; I missed not one tortured movement, neither word, nor forgiving prayer. I watched Him die, tormented by the demons He cast out of me. My Jesus! And now I seek His body and find it not—as if He never was. As if it were a dream. As if He never touched me, healed me, loved me, and compelled me to lay down my sin.

Poor Mary! She knew He was dead; she'd
*   watched Him die,*
Hanging between earth and sky.
She knew He was dead; she'd heard Him scream
As the filth of our sin had come in between,
Himself and His God, as the punishment rod
Fell to chastise His choicest prize.
She knew He was dead, so pardon her
For thinking Him only the gardener!
He called her name; He was just the same,
Save the holes in His hands and His spear-
*   pierced frame.*
The love and fire in His eyes were too much,
The strength and the thrill of His risen-life
*   touch.*
Dear Lord! Dear Lord! Oh, pardon her
For thinking you only the gardener!
Many folks that I know have a Jesus of gloom,
Alive, yet confined to His garden tomb.
Yes, He came alive, but was never the same,
He never called them by their very own name!
He lives in His tomb and He tends His grave,

Confined and helpless to seek and to save.
Look into His face, let go of His feet,
Stop trying to wrap Him in that winding sheet!
He isn't the gardener, a ghost, or a fake,
He's Rabboni, your Master and He rose for
*   your sake.*
What will you do with Jesus who is called

GARDEN OF GETHSEMANE

Christ? Will you wash your hands and stain your soul, or will you refuse a confrontation with this just man? Will you, angered by His silence, cover up His person with a dark cloak of mockery and scorn? Or will you, like the soldier, recognize that it was you who crucified the Son of God and fearlessly voice it to the world? Are you a disciple of the night, burying with reverence in your tomb of doubt the great teacher you had hoped was God? Or are you a disciple of the day, convinced He is alive because you met Him in your garden of despair? The choice is yours; for, whatever you do with Jesus who is called Christ, God will let you do.

"*A happiness that does not depend upon happenings happening to happen the way a person happens to want them to happen is a happiness worth pursuing!*"

Happiness Is

Feelings! What a huge part they play in all of our lives. My husband was talking about the illusive feelings of happiness that people seek and he put it this way: "If their happenings happen to happen the way they happen to want them to happen, then they'll be happy!" The sensation of happiness that so many are chasing can be indeed a most illusive thing! Some people think their happiness lies in the secular events of their calendar and so fill their days with busyness which leaves them barren and listless with trying to keep up! This dependence upon secular happenings is superficial and rarely lasts longer than the events in question.

Some people look for happiness elsewhere. They search for it in the sentimental instead of the secular and buy up all the delightful Charles Shultz books that tell them "Happiness is a warm puppy." Sentimental happiness lasts just about as long as the puppy behaves itself on the lounge rug! If we allow our happiness to be dictated by dates and dogs, we will find the waves of happy emotion lapping our lives as spasmodically and unpredictably as the incoming waves of the sea! Others feel they have an inalienable right to happiness; they point out that even our country's great Constitution tells us that everyone has the right to life, liberty, and the pursuit of happiness! They feel the country owes them the opportunity to find happiness anywhere at any price. In other words, they believe their search for personal gratification is "sanctioned" by the government! "Everyone and everything exists for my benefit," they tell us, "for I have a perfect right to be happy." It is about this pursuit of personal peace and joy that I write.

On resurrection day, two of the disciples were walking along the road to a small village called Emmaus. They were turning their backs upon some very distressing events that had destroyed their happiness. The Bible tells us that they were sad because their happenings had not happened to happen the way they happened to "hope" they would happen!

"We *hoped* that it had been He (Jesus) who *should have* redeemed Israel, . . . " they sadly confided to the mysterious stranger who had joined them on their journey (Luke 24:21). I think we can well relate to the disciples' dilemma, for much of our own hoped-for happiness has been wrapped up in events that we felt should have happened and never did! There have been things we banked on that have not materialized and dreams we dreamed that have never solidified from fantasies once they saw the light of day!

"Happiness is a tall, dark, handsome football player who will ask me to homecoming," dreams the little cheerleader as she prances and dances on the sidelines. But he doesn't and so happiness is not! Happiness is that special trip we will take this summer, says the young and harrassed mother; but the hoped-for exotic journey is too expensive, and the mundane vacation in the usual place is spoiled because of the thoughts of the trip that might have been. Happiness is good health, believes the chronically ill; it is marriage, sighs the single person; it is motherhood, decides the barren one. Happiness is accomplishment, says the pianist as she practices hard; it is popularity, says the one who is continually shunned. Yes, for some, happiness is part and parcel of what has NEVER HAPPENED, but hopefully can be manipulated to happen in the future! "But wait a minute," some of you might say, "that has not been so in *my* case. Things, events, people, and places *have* brought me happiness. The waves of contentment have lapped consistently upon my shores and there have been marvelous times of fulfillment and joy." In other words, you are telling me that you are not walking along sadly as the disciples walked, but rather skipping along the shoreline of life with great jubilation! Things *have* happened to happen the way you've happened to want them to happen! Well, that's good; and I'm glad you are celebrating. But I submit to you, your happiness STILL depends on happenings, and I would like to ask you just what will happen to your heart if those marvelous things or that beautiful person upon which your feelings depend are taken away from you?

For many, happiness depends upon people and how those people can stimulate and satisfy their bodily appetites. For them, happiness is not so much linked to the secular or the sentimental event as to sensual experience. "Happiness is a good rock concert," comments a high school kid "in love" with the leader of the band. "Boy, does that music turn me on!" For others, happiness is a malt, or a huge steak, beer, drugs, or sex. The problem with this sort of happiness is that it isn't very permanent. The happiness connected with our sensual appetites lasts for a few hours at the most and then

depends upon a repetition of the experience, which doesn't always happen to happen!

Sometimes we meet a wonderful person and grow to love him exclusively. The whole of our life and the meaning of our existence is centered around him and all our hopes and dreams are gathered together in a bundle and laid in his lap. What a traumatic thing then when he dies, leaves home, or is removed from our lives. But let's think about a far greater crisis that can arise if the one we love doesn't die or disappear, but disappoints us instead. There is nothing that smothers happiness more than being disappointed in someone you really had trusted. Those two men walking along that dusty road in Jesus' day knew all about that! "We had hoped that it had been He who should have redeemed Israel," they lamented! They did indeed feel most grievously cheated.

One of the worst sorts of unhappiness is the disenchantment we can experience when we have once been deliriously happy and then suddenly find our world falling apart. When we have put the whole of our faith in someone and he doesn't, or can't come through, then we are unhappy indeed! A wife who has been rejected knows all about this, as does a passed-over boyfriend, an abandoned child, or even an employer who has had to dismiss, for misconduct, a man whom he hired and believed in. "We were so *sure* we could trust them," we say, "and then, then they let us down." Can you imagine the depression those two disciples were experiencing on that day so long ago? How desperately unhappy they must have been. How did they cope with it? First, they did what disappointed people do best when they are hurting; they found someone with the same problem and were sharing their misery by having a pity party. "And they talked together of all these things which had happened. And it came to pass that, while they communed together and reasoned . . ." (Luke 24:14, 15). As soon as happiness flies away we fly away, too, anyplace, anywhere, to find solace! Who would understand us, we wonder frantically as we find that unbelievable note on the kitchen table telling us our husband is never coming back, our child has left home, or someone has had a terrible

"God's 'soul joy' will chase [them] through the years, in and out of all circumstances and situations and all conceivable relationships, insisting on singing a song in the soul and setting it on fire with eternal joy!"

accident. We run to a neighbor or a friend who may be able to blow on the dying embers of our happiness and kindle the flame anew. We seek out someone who has had the same terrifying trauma thrust upon him and has survived to tell the tale! I have noticed we do not run easily to the One who is the Source of all happiness, but usually to one who is also unhappy!

Secondly, we do not find these particular disciples praying about their problem but simply perpetuating it by endlessly going over and over the details. It may be that in the sudden sense of loss they were experiencing, prayer was too impossible to contemplate, or too sweet to stand. Maybe the death of all their dreams necessitated a careful avoidance of the Almighty who they inwardly felt could surely have prevented the catastrophe from happening in the first place! The disciples' greatest confusion must have concerned the silence of the Lord God. How was it that He, who thundered from heaven on the Mount of Transfiguration, "This is my beloved Son, hear Him," said a mighty "nothing" on the Mount of Calvary to those who were crucifying Him? They had hoped that Jesus was God's man, sent from God's heaven, to do God's work; and therein lay the dashing of all their hopes in the shape of the cross. To be disappointed in people is one thing, but to be disappinted in God is another! They had spent three years following a man they believed was divine. They had left loved ones, business, and home and had "trusted" that it was "He!" No wonder, in the days following Calvary, they "walked and were sad!"

Some of us have known what it is to trust people and have learned our lessons concerning their fallibility. We have come to be more careful with our hearts. Others of us have come to a bitter (and always wrong) conclusion that God is not to be trusted either. We believe He has let us down and has not come through on His word. We have expected Him to save us and have found ourselves instead in a dreadful Gethsemane of our own. I have discovered that the great unhappiness caused by this spiritual disillusionment can only be healed by the living Christ Himself. The deepest and most intense emotions we can experience as human beings

are not sensual or secular but *spiritual* ones, and they go deeper into our psyches than any other feeling. They have to do with the "heart" of man, that inner part of us that cannot be tickled by sand, stimulated by loud music, or assuaged by food, drink, or sex. These spiritual senses were the very ones with which the two disciples were grappling on the road to Emmaus.

In other words, our deepest and truest happiness depends on what occurs deep down in our innermost soul. We talk in the popular vernacular of "soul" longings or "soul" music, and we know what we mean when we talk of such things. Think about the "soul" agony of the disciples as they were communing and reasoning about the spiritual events of those last few days. They must have felt that they had run the gamut of emotions by the time resurrection day dawned. We read that they had been amazed and astonished by the reports of the resurrection from the dead that the women brought to them. Having closely ques-

tioned them, however, and having discovered that, despite their excited chatter, the women had "seen Him not," the disciples experienced the deflating of their bubble of expectation (Luke 24:24).

They must have been experiencing a certain amount of guilt as well, as they talked of their defection at the trial of Jesus and their "non-presence" at the cross. Now, as they walked away from Jerusalem toward their homes and loved ones, there must have been a certain apprehension about picking up the pieces again after months of ministry with Jesus. Yes, feelings are funny things when they rule our lives and our reactions. *Facts* are the anchor that we need to keep us stable in such circumstances!

Jesus (who had been their strange and mysterious companion on the road, although they knew Him not) decided it was time to share some of His own feelings with His sad friends! His were feelings of frustration at these "foolish ones" who had been "so slow of heart to believe all that the prophets had spoken" (Luke 24:25.) He was explaining to them that their happiness had to depend on what they believed about *Him* and not on what happened to them!

> Ought not Christ to have suffered these things and to enter into his glory? And beginning at Moses and all the prophets, he expounded unto them, in all the scriptures, the things concerning Himself.
>
> Luke 24:26, 27

A human being has the grand ability to be happy, soul happy. Obviously, the only way soul satisfaction can be obtained is when close contact is made with the soul Maker. To place our trust in a man, or in a woman, or in a boy or girl can have happy or unhappy results, depending on the worth of the person in whom we put our trust. But, since every person is fallen and fallible and most certainly mortal, by the law

"Lo, I am with you alway, even unto the end of the world" (Matt. 28:20).

of averages we are all in for some unhappy days. What if my faith and trust and my yearning heart that longs to be truly content could be placed in the hands of the One who is perfect goodness and love? Then surely my happiness would be a stable thing. God is such a One. He is the *only* One who can be absolutely trusted with our vulnerable hearts. Walking along that lonely path 2,000 years ago, two men sensed their companion had the clue to their deep distress. They decided to pursue their conversation and constrained Him to stay with them that night.

> And it came to pass, as he sat eating with them, he took bread, and blessed it, and broke it, and gave it to them. And their eyes were opened, and they recognized him; and he vanished out of their sight. And they said one to another, Did not our heart burn within us, while he talked with us along the way, and while he opened to us the scriptures?

> Luke 24:30-32.

I wonder if it was the nail prints that did it. As Christ broke the bread in that heart-catchingly familiar way and passed it to them, they would have seen the awful holes in His hands; and suddenly they must have known that they had not placed their hopes in the wrong person after all. Jesus of Nazareth was indeed God incarnate, the Messiah, the One the prophets had promised would come to be the eternal source of happiness forever. If we are to know a joy that lasts, we have to "talk with Him along the way" as Cleophas and his friend did. We will have to let Him open the scriptures to us and allow Him to explain the things concerning Himself. This doesn't mean an occasional journey through a church door on the Sabbath, or a once-in-a-while contribution in the collection plate, or a Christmas carol sung with the neighbors once a year. This expounding will take time and energy. It will mean we start to study the Bible for ourselves and seek to understand the Old Testament scriptures and how they speak of Christ our Savior. Remember that the Bible study the Lord Jesus shared on that occasion was taken from the Old Testament, the New not yet having been written!

This description of spiritual happiness says it all. The unbelieving, cold, unhappy hearts were touched by the resurrected Christ and were warmed by heaven's joy. This is the sort of happiness that lasts, but it is also the sort of joy that provokes and pushes us from within to share our joy with others. Although the day was far spent, those disciples on the way to Emmaus,

> . . . rose up the same hour, and returned to Jerusalem, and found the eleven gathered together, and those who were with them, saying, The Lord is risen indeed, and hath appeared to Simon. And they told what things were done along the way, and how he was known to them in the breaking of bread.

> Luke 24:33-35

A happiness that does not depend upon happenings happening to happen the way a person happens to want them to happen is a happiness worth pursuing! Not only is it worth pursuing, but once caught, it will begin to pursue him! God's "soul joy" will chase him through the years, in and out of all circumstances and situations and all conceivable relationships, insisting on singing a song in the soul and setting it on fire with eternal joy!

Finally, we read that Christ, after breaking bread, "vanished" out of their sight. Doesn't it seem that for Him to have disappeared at that point would have tumbled them right back into the pit of unhappiness all over again? But it didn't! Not one whit disturbed, they set off to return to Jerusalem, even though the hour was ridiculously late, to tell their brother disciples that they had seen the Lord. The fact that He disappeared as He did only proved His power to them, for who but God could do such things? Since He was indeed divine, they knew He would be with them always, in all places *whether they could see Him or not*! That is the reason that spiritual joy is so very different from happiness that depends on happenings; for it rejoices instead in the diety of Christ and in a sure and steady trust in His promise that He will indeed abide with us forever! "Lo," He said, "Lo, I am with you alway, even unto the end of the world!" (Matt. 28:20).

"... will ye therefore that I release unto you the King of the Jews? Then cried they all again, saying, Not this man, but Barabbas. Now Barabbas was a robber" (John 18:39b, 40).

"Now Barabbas Was a Robber"

There was no question about it; Barabbas was a robber. The gospel of Mark tells us that not only was the man a robber, but he was also a murderer. We do not know if he was a political animal or simply a hired assassin, but it is clear from the scripture text that he had been connected with a revolt against the Romans (Mark 15:7). Maybe he was a robber and a murderer because he was a political activist, or maybe he was a robber and a murderer because he was a robber and a murderer! Some people are born bad, some say! But do you really believe that some are born sinners and others not? Have you ever wondered what it is that makes a man break the law? The Bible tells us that there is something drastically wrong with the human race and that man has a propensity to break the moral code. We are told that every man, woman, and child comes into this world with a bias to sin within them.

I used to live in England. In the park on a Sunday afternoon, Grandpa and Grandma would turn out dressed in their Sunday best to play the game of bowls. It all looked quite easy until one day I tried it. Grandpa showed me how. Bending down, he rolled the small white ball called a jack across the crew-cut lawn. Then he told me the object of the exercise was to roll the big, black bowl as near the little, white jack as I could without letting the two touch. Well, that looked simple enough, I thought. But simple it was not. However straight I would aim that black bowl at that little, white blob, away it would veer on a pathway all of its own! Something was obviously tugging it off course. Laughingly, Grandpa explained to me that within the black bowl there was a "bias," a weight, set off-center, that had the effect of pulling the bowl off track every time! Therein lay the art of the game!

Sin is like that weight and man is like the bowl. He is born with a bias. You can aim a man as straight as it is possible to aim him at the desired goal but watch and see how the "sin principle" within tries to pull him off course every time. So what is it that makes a man break the law? His sinful nature. To sin simply means not to keep God's rules or wishes; in other words, to come short of His expected standards.

Some people become very upset if anyone suggests a little baby is born with a moral defect. They insist wrongdoing is a learned skill; the child "apes" its parents or peers, and thereby becomes contaminated. Now there is no question that parents, peers, and environment can have an incredible influence on a child, but I think back to our own babies and I

"... if we have ever been angry with someone or ever robbed anyone ... our teachers of time at school, our employers of time at work, or our parents of their right to restrain and discipline us, ... we have fallen short of ... God's standard of perfection."

can assure you I did not teach them to be disobedient, or to scream in selfish temper tantrums when thwarted, or to answer back, or tell a little lie or two. No one else sneaked into our home and taught them how to do all that, either. They seemed to know instinctively just how best to come short of our standards. It was as if it were all second nature to them which, of course, as a Christian, I believe it was; for I accept the explanation of scripture that we were all "born sinners!"

But what is this standard that God expects of us, you may ask? And if I have been born with a bias of evil within my heart, how can God expect me to attain such a standard anyway? In fact, that doesn't even sound very fair of God to expect me to live up to His standards when He knows about this principle of sin inside of me that pulls me away from right action.

First of all, the standard He expects is perfection. "Be ye perfect as your Father in heaven is perfect!" Christ said. But how does such perfection behave, you may ask? It is summed up in the keeping of the rules God gave to Moses. He told him to write them down for us so we would know exactly what we should do and what we are aiming for! We have to be able to see the white jack to even know if we are heading in the right direction! Two of the things that He told us were wrong were robbing and killing. If we do those things we are definitely heading in the wrong direction. He tells us in Exodus 20:13, 15, "Thou shalt not kill. . . . Thou shalt not steal."

There are some very primitive societies that extol killing and robbing as virtues. It is very hard for us to comprehend such things, but it is so. In tribes where such attitudes are the norm, a murderer who "fattens" a victim with friendship and then kills and eats his unsuspecting friend is held in almost holy awe and reverence! When a missionary first went to these people with the story of the Christian gospel, they chose Judas as their hero instead of Jesus! They had their own laws, they had their own standards, and they had decided what was right and wrong for them. But there is only one absolutely right way, and we believe

Christ came to live it and to tell us about it. He came to explain that whatever a man decides is right or wrong is really irrelevant if he reasons from the basis of his own human wisdom, because God has already told us the truth and it isn't a matter of man's speculation but rather of God's revelation. The Bible teaches us that there is an absolute standard that has already been revealed; but because of sin within us all, we have been pulled aside and have not attained it nor even wanted to attain it! "All have sinned and come short of the glory of God," Romans 3:23 says; and again the scripture says, "There is none righteous, no not one." Yes, if we know our own hearts, we have to admit we are not only sinners by nature, but sinners by choice!

"Well," you say, "I am not a murderer. I've never killed anyone." When Jesus was on earth He explained to us that when we become angry with someone without cause it could lead to terrible violence, which in turn could lead to dreadful crimes of homicide (Matt. 5:21, 22). If you are angry, that's the same as committing the actual murder, He told us, for anger is the root from which the fruit of murder finds its expression. So if we have ever been angry with someone or ever robbed anyone—not of material things perhaps, but maybe our teachers of time at school, our employers of time at work, or our parents of their right to restrain and discipline us—we will have to admit we have fallen short of the standard: God's standard of perfection.

Barabbas certainly had fallen far short of that standard of perfection, for he had robbed and he had killed and had been apprehended and bound in prison for it. I'm sure everyone agrees Barabbas was a sinner and that Barabbas deserved all that was coming to him.

But it is much easier to agree that Barabbas was a sinner than to admit that we are! The Bible says we are like Barabbas for we have robbed God. We have robbed Him of our worship, our service, our money, and our time. We have stolen our love and our praise from Him to whom it was due and lavished it on others and on ourselves. If we look honestly into our own hearts, we will have to admit we have also been angry many times without cause. Our sin is no different than the sin of Barabbas. He just committed more of it, that's all. The circumstances of his environment and the cultural factors and enormous pressures of his day and age all helped play a part in pushing him to the extreme of this sin; but without a doubt, we stand as Barabbas stood before the bar of heaven and can know as surely as he knew that we are found as guilty as he!

The Bible says we are indeed condemned already. "What do you mean, already?" you may ask. I mean we are already condemned by God for falling short of His ten heavenly moral demands; and what is more, we have been doing it all of our lives. We often call our sins our shortcomings, as if they are sweet, endearing characteristics that we have freely forgiven ourselves for. Actually, "shortcomings" are not little aspects of our particular personality at all, but are rather "coming shorts" and are anything but endearing to God. They are, in fact, big, ugly things that God has condemned already. Now everyone who sins is a sinner just as surely as everyone who swims is a swimmer!

Committing a sin simply proves the nature of the tree. "What is in must come out," as the saying goes! The heart of man is deceitful above all things and desperately wicked, says the Good Book. "Well, I don't agree," I can hear an exasperated mother of four saying. "If it weren't for my kids I'd be the sweetest thing imaginable. My children get me so riled up it's ridiculous!" What she is saying is, "It's my children's fault I lose my temper, not mine!" Or to put it another way, "My kids create my spirit." Not so, children don't create your spirit; they reveal it. That's right! A cupful of sweet water cannot spill one bitter drop, even when it's jogged. The picture of the human heart is not a very pretty one when God paints it. "Out of the heart of man proceed evil thoughts, murders, adulteries, fornications, thefts, false witness, blasphemies" (Matt. 15:19).

So the point is this: Barabbas was a sinner, but so are we! He needed to be saved from the repercussions of his sin, and so do we. Barabbas found himself bound by his sin, and so do we. There are few of us arrogant and dishonest enough to profess to have no binding habit that needs loosing in our lives. There is no man on the face of the earth who doesn't need to be saved from at least one thing! Barabbas was also in prison. He was in prison because he had been caught, tried, convicted, and condemned; and so in a sense are we. The Bible teaches that we have broken God's laws and we have been caught doing it—caught by the lawgiver Himself who has already pronounced judgment upon us.

Now it is very hard for respectable robbers to believe they are condemned by God, especially religious robbers who regularly go to church. They think the penalty for sin is going to church on Sunday, or getting rid of their small change in the offering plate when it comes by, or saying their prayers, or reading their Bible. The penalty for sin is none of these things. I know many people who do all those things, and while they are doing them, they certainly look and possibly think they are paying their penalties. But the Bible says the penalty of sin is not the performance of religious activities but rather death! One million visits to church could never pay for one single sin against God. Ten million fervent prayers could never pay the debt I owe to the Almighty for my misdoings. No, the wages of sin is death and only death will do! I remember being stopped by a rather irate policeman who asked for my driving license and informed me I had been speeding. I had broken the law and had to pay a speeding fine. Can you imagine his face if I had offered to attend church instead! Attending church would certainly be helpful *after* the event to remind me not to break the law again, but nothing would appease the law other than the required penalty. It is a sad and terrible thing that our churches are full of unforgiven robbers who think their religious exercises will *commute* their sentences. Not so, the sentence has already been passed on all of us and somebody needs to pay the prescribed penalty. But wait a moment! What happened to Barabbas?

Now at that feast he released unto them one prisoner, whomsoever they desired. And there was one named Barabbas, who lay bound with them that had made insurrection with him, who had committed murder in the insurrection. . . . And Pilate answered, and said again unto them, What will ye, then, that I shall do unto him whom ye call the King of the Jews? And they cried out again, Crucify him! Then Pilate said unto them, Why, what evil hath he done? And they cried out the more exceedingly, Crucify him! And so Pilate, willing to content the people, released Barabbas unto them, and delivered Jesus, when he had scourged him, to be crucified.

Mark 15:6-15

I can just imagine Barabbas lying in his cell waiting for that fateful sound of the bolt being drawn back on his door. I'm sure he had been able to see the Romans constructing the crude wooden crosses that he and his accomplices would soon be crucified upon. He would have noticed with a certain gruesome and grim satisfaction that his cross was the largest and most important looking instrument of all. As the soldiers came to get him, Barabbas must have tensed his tired and battered body against the restraining ropes that cruely bit into his flesh as he lay huddled on the mud floor and said to himself, "This is it!" But to his amazement the door was thrown open; and as the light shone in, a grim soldier must have roughly jerked him to his feet and with a sharp knife cut his bonds away. "You're a lucky devil," he probably muttered. "Off you go and don't let us catch you again or next time you won't be alive to tell the tale, I can promise you!"

I'm sure Barabbas followed the crowd of sightseers along the narrow streets and outside the city walls to Calvary. There was a man on his cross. Yes, there was! And yet he mustn't have recognized him. As Barabbas looked into his face, he probably had never seen Him before in his life. He would have known every robber and murderer and rascal for miles around, so I can imagine him asking himself who it could be? Pushing closer, for I'm sure his curiosity got the better of him, he would have been able to read the inscription the soldiers were nailing over the crucified man's head. "This is the King of the Jews!" it said. What did it all mean to Barabbas? I'm sure he didn't know. How confused he must have been.

He may have noticed a man and woman standing close to him. The woman was fainting and obviously a close relative of the man on the cross, and the victim was telling the man to look after her for him. He would have caught the words "son" and "mother" and looked again at the man supporting the woman. Can't you believe he would have wanted to ask, "Who is that man on the center cross?" And can't you just hear John's reply, "That is Jesus Christ; He is the Son of God. He made the blind to see, the dumb to speak, the lame to walk. He is a good man and I don't know why He hangs between the earth and heaven. I don't know why He dies!" So saying, he perhaps looked desperately at Barabbas as if demanding an explanation from him. Barabbas, looking into the eyes of his Savior, could have answered, "I don't know why He dies either; all I know is He has taken my place. He hangs on my cross; He's bearing my punishment and because He dies, I live!" Barabbas had been saved! That was for sure! He had not been saved because he deserved it, but simply because the Son of God bore his sins in His own body on the tree and died in his place. Barabbas's murder was paid for by Christ, as surely as every sin you and I have ever committed was paid for, as well, by our blessed substitute: the Lord Jesus Christ.

I remember hearing this illustration when I was eighteen years of age. I had just come to realize I was a robber! I had stolen my life and lived it as if it were mine for eighteen years. I was not aware someone had paid a price for it and I was not my own. I came to God and asked Him for Christ's sake to forgive me and He did. Like Barabbas, I simply admitted I was a sinner, coming far short of the standard set for me. Like Barabbas, I believed I was sentenced and awaiting judgment by a just judge who had condemned me already. And like Barabbas, I metaphorically climbed a hill and knelt at a cross and told Jesus I didn't understand it all, but I realized He had died *in my* place, on my cross *as my* substitute. I thanked Him for life, new life, resurrection life. And after a while, I began to notice something. Robbers who have been forgiven much, love much; and even robbers can be changed!

" . . . not my will, but thine, be done" (Luke 22:42b).

When the Right Feeling Is Wrong

I remember discovering that our children had not been born with "a will" but rather with "a won't." If I said yes, they said no; if I said no, they said yes. Looking back, the whole of that initial child rearing period seemed to be comprised of a battle of the wills. Not long ago, as I watched a two-year-old tussling with his father, I was again reminded that a baby is born with a full-grown will! It's amazing how body size has nothing at all to do with it and that the will of the little fellow matches up perfectly with Mom's and Dad's as soon as the toddler toddles. Likewise, the will of a child of God clashes with the heavenly Father's wishes. He says no, we say yes; He says yes, we say no! All our Christian lives there is a battle.

For eighteen years I had lived quite happily with the philosophy "My will, not thine, be done," for to live selfishly required no battle at all. After I had given my life to Christ, however, I was surprised to discover I needed daily to wage war to want what He wanted! I soon learned that since I had become a Christian, I needed to begin to practice saying, "Not *my* will, but *Thine*, be done." Even after I had been a practicing Christian for some time, I still found it hard not to want my own way; but I did notice that something had changed within me. Now there was no freedom or happiness in planning my life or doing my own thing. Unless I was *in* the will of God and busy *doing* the will of God, I was miserable and out of step with life.

It all began when I discovered that my relationship with God required active belief. The girl who helped me come to know Christ had not asked me, "Do you believe?" She inquired, instead, "*Will* you believe?" Everybody is a believer, she informed me. We all believe in something. It is the object of our belief, or our faith, that is important. I did believe in Jesus Christ and that He was the Son of God, but all that was in my head and had to do with my mind, not my will. If I had been asked at that time, "*Do* you believe?" I would have answered "Yes, of course." But I was not asked that. I was asked instead *will* you believe *into* Jesus? *Will* you give up your will and yield it into His hands? *Will* you trust yourself, abandon yourself, to Him? *Will* you, in other words, put your head belief and your heart feeling into willing action? The will is the part of us that moves us to *do* the very thing we have become intellectually convinced that we should. We are made up of body, soul, and spirit. Some say that the soul is our personality and is comprised of our mind, our emotions, and our will. All three need to be in motion for a true conversion to take place.

First of all, there is our mind. This critical faculty that we all possess has the ability to examine facts and understand the import of them. Where the Christian gospel is concerned, some theological ideas about God need to be absorbed and considered. The Bible makes categorical claims about the Almighty's holiness and man's great sinfulness. It tells us that God has eyes too pure to look on iniquity and that our sins have caused a great "divorce" between us and our Maker. The Bible record continues to explain that a marriage between Christ as the heavenly bridegroom and forgiven sinners who have become part of his body, or bride, is possible to bring this terrible separation to an end. God made that reconciliation a reality at the cross. Our minds need to consider carefully these facts and to come to an intelligent conclusion. It is at this point that the emotions come into play and are often touched. I didn't say always, I said often. Sometimes it is an overwhelmingly emotional thing to hear the story of Jesus, and people can be deeply moved with a great desire to respond to God after they have come to understand the size of His sacrifice for them. Sometimes, instead of an emotion of sorrow, a person is overcome with a deep sense of contrition, or a shamed sense of duty, that makes him want to try to put the wrong thing right. Emotions of one sort or another usually play *some* part in our coming to faith, but this is the least important part of the process and need not necessarily play any part at all! With the mind convinced and the emotions touched, it is now left to the will to decide. At this point it is superfluous to ask, "Do you believe?" for we have already established that fact! The big question is now, *will* you believe *into* Jesus, or rather *will* you trust yourself wholly to Him and to His finished work of redemption on your behalf? *Will* you say, in effect, "From this time forth, by your grace, I will say 'Not *my will*, but *thine*, be done' "?

A successful Christian life is the life that starts on this premise and continues to run on these principles. No one said it is going to be easy! Listen to Jesus agonizing over it in Gethsemane, "O my Father, if it be possible, let this cup pass from me; nevertheless, not as I will, but as thou wilt" (Matt. 26:39). Scoffield notes that the "cup" must be interpreted by our Lord's own use of that symbol in speaking of His approaching sacrificial death. Jesus did not want to die, no more than do we! "Greater love hath no man than this," said Jesus, "that a man lay down his life for his friends" (John 15:13). Our Lord demonstrated His great love for us by dying when He didn't want to die.

To do the will of God undoubtedly means often doing what we do not want to do! It will mean a constant crucifixion of selfishness. "I die daily," said the apostle Paul, and I believe that this is what he meant. If we could only start to practice such a lifestyle, imagine the blessing that would result. We would daily lay down our lives for our friends. We would think of them first and ourselves last. We would serve their needs and not our own. We would be available to people we don't want to be available to and help people we don't want to help. Many of *my* world's problems would be solved if only HIS WILL, NOT MINE, would start to be done. I said "*my* world's" problems because "*my* world" is really all I shall be held personally accountable for. "My world" may be my own home and my own children, or it may be my own neighborhood; then again it may be a little larger. It could be that my world will stretch across the sea to other men's worlds. But my world will certainly be the sphere of *my* influence, and, whatever its boundaries, I need to know the will of God and what He would have me do, starting just where I am!

The first thing I need to do is to exercise that will of mine, come to Christ and give Him everything, including my mind, my emotions, and my will, and then continue to obey Him daily, seeking to know and do His pleasure. Sometimes to go on to do the will of God in our particular world will lead to distress, as the Lord Jesus discovered in the garden of Gethsemane. As Christ faced the will of God, we are told, He became very depressed. "My soul is exceeding sorrowful unto death," He told His friends. Nevertheless, He prayed to His Father "not as I will but as Thou wilt!" (Mark 14:34, 39). Jesus was not struggling to *find* the will of

God; He was struggling to *do* it! Sometimes we pretend we do not know what God wants us to do and I think we need to admit that we are being less than honest at those times. The truth of the matter is, we do know, but we don't want to do what we know is right. Jesus knew what He had to do, for there was no doubt in His mind that the time had come to fulfill the will of His heavenly Father and die on the cross. When He celebrated the passover supper with His disciples in the upper room, He prayed, "Father the hour is come, glorify thy Son that thy Son may glorify Thee" (John 17:1). He knew full well that the hour had come, and He knew exactly what He had to accomplish in that hour.

When the will of God is understood and is a depressing and distressing thing, the battle is in exerting the human will to do it. We love ourselves so much, we run from cost and conflict. In the past, I have been asked to talk to church groups about the subject of prayer and fasting. I believe God expects us to engage in those holy exercises, for He did not say "if you fast" but rather "when you fast" (Matt. 6:16). Whenever I finish that particular talk, I receive an interesting response. A lady approached me one day and said, "But I tried fasting, and I got a headache!"

"So what did you do?" I asked.

"Well," she explained slightly flustered, "when I got the headache, I decided I'd better stop."

"Why?" I inquired.

"Well, because it hurt!" she answered somewhat defensively.

The problem is, we all tend to live our lives according to what is physically comfortable instead of what is spiritually profitable! We know it is good for our body to exercise but it makes us hot and sticky, or we get a pain in our side, or it hurts, so we don't! We know it is good for our spirits to pray and to fast but we get a headache, so we don't, or we won't! It is at this point we need to exert the will that has been given to Him and exercise it Godward instead of selfward! It is exactly at this time of struggle that we need to say "Not my will, but Thine, be done," and do it!

Perhaps there is a relationship in our life that needs attention, or there may be a bad business situation that needs setting to rights. There could be some sin in our life that no one knows about, and to repent and confess it will mean restitution, which could result in all sorts of people getting very upset. Even the thought of that is depressing and distressing to us, yet we know it is His will and, therefore, the right thing to do. Will you say, "Not my will, but Thine be done?" and go and do it? If you are a follower of Christ, you must.

Sometimes a young person finds himself at a party where everyone is drinking too much. He sees his friends getting drunk and then begins to be pressured to do the same. Perhaps that young person feels that his Christian commitment has called for him to abstain from drinking at all in this particular situation. "If it feels good, it must be right," teases a friend offering a drink. "Come on," chides another. "You're a big boy now. Surely you're *ready* for some booze." But it isn't a question of whether or not he is *ready*; it's a question of whether or not it is *right*! It isn't a question either of having the attitude that if a thing feels good it must be all right. Eating ice cream feels great to me and would continue to feel good after I'd waded through the third gallon (especially if it were butter pecan), but there would come a moment when I would have to say no to my appetites and stay hungry and do the right thing. I think of the Lord feeling famished after His long fast in the wilderness. "Why don't you use your freedom and power to turn these stones into bread and satisfy your natural appetites?" sug-

gested Satan. But Jesus chose to say no, to do the will of God not the will of Satan (or of His stomach) and to stay hungry!

Perhaps you are a single woman. You feel romatically pulled toward a man in the office, or someone you've met at a social gathering. "If it feels so good, it must be right," you say; but the problem is he's married! The right thing to do has already been clearly stated in the Bible. *And so you can know that that "right" feeling is wrong* in this instance. That natural hunger must be denied if you are to do the thing that pleases Him. You need to choose to stay hungry as Jesus chose to in the Judean wilderness. Now this can certainly be a distressing and depressing thing! Sometimes the will of God will mean you will feel very, very depressed indeed. At such times you may know He fully understands, for the Bible tells us He has been there before and knows just how it is.

But don't misunderstand. The will of God is not always a depressing and distressing thing. It may be so for a season, but always there will be the accompanying joy of knowing that we do His will. This is a deeper experience than a mere emotion; it lies in the area of our spirit and gives a sense of serenity and rest even when to do the will of God requires a cross. There are other times when the will of God will not be a difficult thing at all but rather a sheer delight. The Lord Jesus Christ tells us of His eternal delight in doing the Father's will, "I delight to do thy will, O my God: yea, thy law is within my heart" (Ps. 40:8). People often say to me, "I don't know how you do what you do; it must be awfully difficult." Some of the things I have done have indeed been awfully difficult, but I have found that even difficult things can be a delight, and there are many more that have been sheer joy. I have found it a delight to tell others about all He has done for me, and I have found happiness in spending hours on the streets and in the drug dives in Europe gossiping the gospel. I have been delighted to be a pastor's wife and discover the satisfaction of serving Jesus in this capacity. I have many times been surprised with joy by duties that have been thought of by others as sheer drudgery. But then these things I speak of have been the will of

"Every individual must find God's particular plan and purpose for him and do it; then there will be a great sense of inner fulfillment."

God for *my* life, in *my* world.

Every individual must find God's particular plan and purpose for him and do it; then there will be a great sense of inner fulfillment for that person. For each it will be a different purpose. The point is first to know and believe that God does have a plan for you and desires that you discover what it is. He has promised that, as He lives out His resurrection life within you, He will give you His mind and His will about it all. But how does His will manifest itself, you may ask? First of all, you will begin to accept the person that you are. He will help you be glad about the way you look, the way you think and act, because *He* has accepted the person that you are. As you come to terms with yourself, accepting that this is how He made you, you will begin to be able to see for which areas of service you have been made to function. He will want you to train your talents; He will want you to polish your abilities and then look around to see where they fit best.

When we want to do the will of God above all else, we will surely be told what it is. God doesn't hear too many prayers like the one the Lord Jesus prayed in Gethsemane. Rather than the Thy-will-not-mine-be-done sort, He hears too many of the my-will-not-Thine-be-done ones. When He finds just one Christian who is obedient, you can be sure He is going to move heaven and earth to make certain that person knows what He wants him to do!

God promises that even if His will at times may be depressing or distressing, it will never be too difficult to understand. In this sure confidence is our delight! How then will we be certain to find our answers in life's troubled choices? First of all we will be led to them through the inner conviction of the Holy Spirit who has given us the mind and heart of Christ Himself.

Secondly, we will find them through the Word of God. If we are seeking to do His will and not our own, we will need to look into the Bible daily. His Word will be a light to our feet and a lamp to our path. Within its sacred pages there will be principles to guide us to right actions. God's will concerning the marriage partnership, for example, is clearly stated. I heard about a pastor in New York who had become so discouraged with the terrible problems among married couples he had changed his marriage service from "till death us do part" to "till divorce us do part." I can tell you plainly, because He tells us explicitly, it is the will of God to leave father and mother and cleave unto your spouse forever. You don't even need to pray for guidance on that one!

Whenever a principle of God's law has been laid down in His Word, it is the will of God because He hasn't changed His mind, and God's Ten Commandments are still His best plan for our best blessing. The problem is that man has looked at God's will laid out for us in God's law and has made up his own ten amendments, every one of which says "My will, not thine, be done!" But God will never contradict His Word, and so we need to be exercising our minds by searching and learning the scriptures so that we can know the mind of God in any given situation. Having found out the right thing to do, by matching it to His word, we then have to pull ourselves into line with His will for us. How do we do this? We do it in prayer. Prayer can be likened to a rope stretching between two ships. God is like a great big battleship and we are like a little dinghy attached to the big boat by the rope. Think about it for minute; if the man in the little boat pulls on the rope, then the small craft will snuggle up alongside the bigger vessel. This way the two boats will sail on together wherever the big boat wills. In the garden of Gethsemane, we see a perfect illustration of this principle. Jesus, in the little boat, used the rope of prayer to pull Himself alongside the big boat. He said, in effect, "Not *my* (the little boat's) will, but *Thine* (the big one's), be done.

But how we abuse prayer. We try continually to tug and pull God around to our point of view or alongside the things we have in mind, or we use our quiet time to tell Him what we'd like Him to do for us. Prayer has to stop being our heavenly shopping list and become the debating chamber of the soul where we can battle out the problem; and then, convinced of His side of the argument, we can concede the point to Him. We have to stop thinking of God

"God is like a great big battleship and we are like a little dinghy attached to the big boat by the rope."

"We must meet Him in the garden of prayer. . . ."

as simply the great "Need-meeter in the sky" and begin to realize He is not there exclusively to meet our needs, but that we are here to meet His!

Jesus told the tired disciples in the Garden of Gethsemane that they needed to watch and pray, not only because their enemies were on the way to arrest Him, but also because Jesus knew they would have to watch their own weak and selfish hearts and learn to control their tired and selfish bodies! There are many enemies outside our lives who will try to distract us from doing the will of God. There will be some who scoff at the Bible and tell us that it contradicts itself or that it cannot give us relevant guidance in this day and age. There will be others who, through books, radio, and television teach their own brand of philosophy saying, in effect, "My will, not thine be done!" The thing to do, they will say, is to live exclusively for Number One.

There is also an enemy within. Self strives to be king and leaps up to respond to those outside who offer us their subtle suggestions as an alternative to a relationship with God. When the soldiers came to arrest Jesus and the cross loomed large on the horizon, the disciples ran away. They didn't want to die. Because the disciples gave in to their bodily demands, they were not prepared for the test of the cross. I sometimes think of the cross as the "I" crossed out. To crucify selfishness is a painful occupation, but a necessary one, and must be practiced continually if the will of God is to be done at all!

And so we need to stay alert and build into our lives a daily time with God. We must meet Him in the garden of prayer to be reminded that we never know if there will be a cross tomorrow, and if there is, we must be prepared. We will find it necessary to hear His Word by reading the scriptures and seeking relevant instructions. Then we will need to move into action, for the will of God does not involve merely spiritual rituals, but requires the flesh to do something active about the things the spirit dictates. Jesus said to Peter, James, and John, "The spirit indeed is willing but the flesh is weak!" (Matt. 26:41). The disciples' flesh was tired in the garden of Gethsemane, but Jesus gave it no option but to stay awake. He didn't say "poor things, you are exhausted, why don't you snooze a little?" He continually returned to their slumbering forms and shook them awake, urging them to crucify the flesh, control their natural desires, and prepare themselves for the battle He knew was just around the corner. Some of you who are reading this chapter have become Christians and have made that initial step of giving your will to Him. You may not know just where to look in the Bible to find some help. Start with the gospels, and you will find your model of the Christian life, the Lord Jesus Christ; and then begin to read the epistles which will tell you how to live as the Christian you have become. When I was young in the faith, I thought if I read the Bible I would need to start at the beginning and read to the end! Needless to say, I found myself buried in Leviticus. I didn't realize then that the Bible is a library of books and one must go to the appropriate section to accommodate one's needs.

Today in this wonderfully free country of ours, there are many people who can help us find and do the will of God. Seek out a godly pastor or eminent Christian who is obviously in touch with the Lord and who could help you if you need to make some important decision. Don't forget to use your God-given common sense, as well, and take into account the circumstances around you. Make sure you are fully cognizant of your talents and abilities and request that God reveal your spiritual gift for spiritual service. Above all, ask yourself some honest questions and give yourself some honest answers. I would suggest asking yourself, "Do I believe the will of God is to first know Him and then to do what He tells me to do? Do I believe He is eager and willing to show me what He has in mind? Will I do the task when He shows me what it is, even if it is distressing and difficult? If I am not willing, will I pray that the Lord make me willing to be made willing?" If you can answer these questions in the affirmative, you will begin to know the delightful joy that speeds as an arrow from heaven straight to your innermost being, as you do the eternally important actions He will certainly make known! "Not I, but Christ!"

"Now the next day, that followed the day of the preparation, the chief priests and Pharisees came together unto Pilate, saying, Sir, we remember that that deceiver said . . . After three days I will rise again. Command, therefore, that the sepulchre be made sure until the third day, lest his disciples come by night and steal him away. . . . Pilate said unto them, Ye have a watch; go your way, make it as sure as ye can. So they went, and made the sepulchre sure, sealing the stone, and setting a watch" (Matt. 27:62-66).

"Sir, We Remember"

"Sir, we remember that the deceiver said..." complained the Pharisees to Pilate. The body of the Lord Jesus Christ was hardly cold, and they were remembering! Somehow His words had grown roots in their minds; and even though they had refused the truth of them, they couldn't forget what Jesus Christ had said; and if THEY were remembering, then they had a good notion others might be doing the same! Everything Jesus was, said, and did was worth remembering. Christ Himself was described by the Apostle John as the *Logos* or the *Word*, which means a thought or a concept and the expression of it. John told us that "In the beginning was the Word and the Word was with God and the Word was God, the same was in the beginning with God" (John 1:1).

So when the Father "spoke" Jesus into the hay at Christmastime, it was a heavenly declaration indeed! Jesus was God's best thought and His last word. Hebrews 1:1 tells us, "God, who at sundry times and in divers manners spoke in time past unto the fathers by the prophets, hath in these last days spoken unto us by his Son." Jesus then, was God's *last* Word for the *last* days.

It's amazing how much of an impact words have on us isn't it? I can remember all sorts of irrelevant words from as far back as my very first days. I can recollect sweet words, harsh words, critical words, suspicious words. I especially remember wise words spoken by good people. Words once born live forever. They never grow old. You cannot annihilate them, stop them from invading your privacy, or chase them away from your mind. You can try, by playing hide and seek or by filling every waking moment with noise and clatter, with loud music or more words, but at some point you will find yourself alone and off guard; and as clear as a bell you will hear the words you least want to remember. If you think of the worth of a word as the worth of a child and the speaking of it as the birth of an eternal event, then perhaps you will understand the importance of it. Each word, conceived in the mind and brought to birth by the circumstance, goes about its work forever. If such is true of human words, then how much more of God's "Logos." Jesus was the very best thought God had for us as He contemplated our sinful dilemma. That thought, conceived in the mind of God for us, brought Christ to birth. Having spoken His Logos in the shape of a Savior, He expected us to take note of His grand and heavenly statement!

The people who lived in Christ's town, in His home, around His countryside and worshiped in His synagogue and temple heard Him

"Beginning even early in His ministry, Jesus had told His disciples 'how he must go unto Jerusalem, and suffer many things of the elders and chief priests and scribes and be killed, and be raised again the third day' " (Matt. 16:21).

speak. At the age of twelve the doctors marveled at His questions. When He was grown, the disciples wondered at His wisdom, and the common people freely acknowledged the authority with which He spoke. Even the dead obeyed His imperatives. Everything He was and did said something of eternal worth; and all that He spoke carried with it that certain quality and consistency of everlasting value, so that they couldn't help remembering. So it was that the Pharisees remembered! At least *they* gave the person and the sayings of Jesus grave, serious, and believing thought. That is more than we can say of some people today.

I was sitting on a plane not long ago and next to me sat a large man with an equally large ego. He regaled all of those within the sound of his voice with stories of his business exploits until we were embarrassed for him! Engaging him in conversation, I tried to talk about Christ. After awhile I asked him, "Have you ever considered Jesus Christ's claims?"

"Quite honestly," he replied, "I haven't given Him a thought!"

"That's really sad," I said, "Jesus was God's best thought and you haven't even spared Him one of yours!"

At least the Pharisees were giving Him all *their* thought the day after they had crucified Him. They were taking His claims very, very seriously indeed. To what exactly were the enemies of Christ referring? They were remembering that Jesus Christ had brought to bouncing birth some words that could not easily be forgotten. He had told them that He knew He would be killed, but that after three days He would rise again. "For as Jonah was three days and three nights in the whale's belly, so shall the Son of man be three days and three nights in the heart of the earth" (Matt. 12:40), He had said. And again, "Destroy this temple, and in three days I will raise it up" (John 2:19).

Beginning even early in His ministry, Jesus had told His disciples "how he must go unto Jerusalem, and suffer many things from the elders and chief priests and scribes and be killed, and be raised again the third day" (Matt. 16:21).

As completely as He could, Christ had sought to prepare His friends for His crucifixion. While they were yet in Galilee He had told them, " 'I am going to be betrayed into the power of those who will kill me, and on the third day afterwards I will be brought back to life again.' And the disciples' hearts were filled with sorrow and dread" (Matt. 17:22, 23 Living Bible). But He also assured them they would see Him again, telling them:

The world will greatly rejoice over what is going to happen to me, and you will weep. But your weeping shall suddenly be turned to wonderful joy (when you see me again). It will be the same joy as that of a woman in labor when her child is born—her anguish gives place to rapturous joy and the pain is forgotten. You have sorrow now, but I will see you again and then you will rejoice; and no one can rob you of that joy.

John 16:20-22 Living Bible

It amazes me, therefore, that when the Lord Jesus was put to death upon the cross, the disciples did *not* remember what He had said concerning His resurrection but the Pharisees did. Perhaps blinding grief, fear, and consternation obliterated His followers' recollections. The Pharisees, however, hardly had the body of Jesus off the cross before *they* remembered, and that is why we find them in front of Pilate pleading for a guard and a seal. I do not think they really believed the disciples were in any fit state to take on the might of Rome and the temple police and steal the body of the Lord Jesus away! I don't believe they feared the disciples at all. Why, the last glimpse they had of them in the Garden of Gethsemane had been a sight of their backs as they had all forsaken Him and fled. No, I am sure they were far more convinced of the veracity of the Word of God and its everlasting elements than the disciples were at this time. In other words, they were frightened out of their minds concerning the resurrection. In their grief the disciples believed Him dead. The Pharisees, on the other hand, having no grief to grapple with, had a clearer vision and were not so sure! They, therefore, reasoned that the thing to do was to seal the tomb and make sure it was "leakproof" or, since they were dealing with "The Word," soundproof. I am sure they were not so much trying to keep the disciples out, as they were seeking to keep the Lord Jesus in.

But how were they to do that? How do you hush up the loudest statement ever made by heaven to earth? What insulation will you use? Well, you can try the method the Pharisees tried if you like and insulate your ears and heart with a rejection of the truth. Jesus claimed to be *the* way, *the* truth and *the* life. He told us no man could come to the Father except by Him. If Jesus Christ *were* God, and God is truth, then Christ could only speak such. He couldn't lie, for that would be contrary to His character. God sent Jesus so that we could receive some straight answers from heaven, and the answers Jesus brought to us might be straight because it is impossible for the truth to give crooked ones. No wonder what He was,

and what He said, was worth remembering. Don't you think that the Pharisees believed that Jesus spoke the truth? They had to believe it because they hired people to tell lies about Him in order to get Him convicted. If they hired them and they paid them, then they *knew* full well who was telling a lie and who wasn't. The biggest reason, I think, that they really believed Jesus was not the deceiver they said he was concerns their fear of the resurrection. Why did they bother to guard the grave and go to the trouble of sealing the tomb tight? Why make it as secure as they possibly could? I believe they believed but had chosen deliberately to reject what they knew to be true.

Now to decide to believe the truth isn't the truth is quite a declaration in itself! Let me apply all this to the reader of these pages. Do you know all about Jesus Christ and His claim

DOOR TO THE GARDEN TOMB

MOUNT OF ASCENSION

to be God? Do you say He was a deceiver, or do you know in your heart He was indeed the ultimate truth? What have *you* done with the "evidence" concerning His diety? The Pharisees had been there, right in front of the tomb when He had raised Lazarus from the dead. They believed *that* all right; they could hardly do otherwise when the whole countryside began flocking to the house of Martha and Mary to gape at the man brought back from the dead. It was *because* of their very belief that they set about to slay Him! The Pharisees show us how lost you can be, if, believing He was who He said He was and therefore spoke the only truth that matters, you seek to murder Him anyway, twisting His words or rejecting His message! Do you believe the Bible is the Word of God as it claims to be? Would you take a pair of scissors and chop the pages out that you cannot accept?

What difference is there between cutting it up with scissors and chopping it up with your tongue?

Many people today call Jesus Christ the deceiver. They say He lied about Himself and sought to deceive the world. We might give credence to their words apart from the fact of the resurrection. But, as Paul wrote, "If Christ be not raised, your faith is vain!" (1 Cor. 15:17). The resurrection proved beyond a shadow of a doubt that Jesus Christ was who He said He was.

It is the Good News about his Son, Jesus Christ our Lord, who came as a human baby, born into King David's royal family line; and by being raised from the dead he was proved to be the mighty Son of God, with the holy nature of God himself.

Romans 1: 3,4 Living Bible

A resurrection from among the dead necessitated the power and dynamics of God. Christ had already demonstrated that power in the raising of Lazarus and had told His enemies He, too, would be raised after three days. The height of the pride and arrogance of man is seen in these verses concerning the Pharisees. Knowing who they were dealing with, they thought themselves capable of fighting, overcoming, and killing God Himself! While you and I are alive we, too, have that dreadfully frightening prerogative. We are perfectly free to examine God's written word and reject it if we wish. We are also free to lock it up, attack it, bury it out of sight, or even crucify it. The problem comes after we are dead because *there will* be a judgment for us whether we choose to believe in one or not, and then we shall face the only one who can raise us up! There was an imaginative and rather chilling piece of dialogue written in an English newspaper that I clipped and kept that puts this thought in rather lucid terms. Let me share it with you:

Genesis

"Who are you?" said the Prime Minister, opening the door.

"I'm GOD" replied the stranger.

"I don't believe you!" sneered the Prime Minister. "Show me a miracle!"

So GOD showed the Prime Minister the miracle of *Birth.*

"Pah!" said the Prime Minister, "My scientists are creating life in test tubes and have nearly solved the secret of heredity. Artificial insemination is more certain than your lackadaisical methods, and by cross breeding we are producing fish and mammals to our design.

"Show me a *proper* miracle!"

And GOD caused the skies to darken and hailstones came tumbling down!

"That's nothing," said the Prime Minister picking up the telephone to the Air Ministry.

"Send up a Met plane, old chap," he said. "And sprinkle the clouds with silver chloride crystals!"

And the Met plane went up and sprinkled the clouds which had darkened the world, and the hailstones stopped pouring down and the sun shone brightly.

"Show me another," said the Prime Minister.

And GOD caused a plague of frogs to descend upon the land.

The Prime Minister picked up his telephone. "Get me the Minister of Agriculture," he said to the operator. "Instruct them to procure a frog killer as myxomatosis killed rabbits."

And soon the land was free from frogs and people gave thanks to the Prime Minister and erected laboratories in his name!

"Show me another!" sneered the Prime Minister.

And GOD caused the sea to divide.

The Prime Minister picked up his direct link telephone to the Polaris Submarine. "Lob a few ICBM's into Antarctica and melt the ice cap, please, old man."

And the ice cap melted and the water and the sea came rushing back.

"I will kill all the firstborn," said GOD.

"Paltry trick," said the Prime Minister, "Watch this!" He pressed a button on his desk and missiles flew to their preordained destinations and H-Bombs slit the world asunder and radioactivity killed every mortal thing!

"I CAN RAISE THE DEAD!" said GOD.

"*Please,*" said the Prime Minister in his coffin, "*Let me live again!*"

"WHY? WHO ARE YOU?" said GOD.

Brian Morris

Man is helpless to raise the dead, because he is only man and cannot impart life. Even the cleverest scientists today cannot create life but can only bring a being into being from life that is already there!

"I am the resurrection and the LIFE," said Jesus of Nazareth and proceeded to prove His point by saying in an authoritive voice, "Lazarus, come forth," and he that was DEAD three days came forth! To have seen this and to have killed the One who did it meant the Pharisees demonstrated a blatant rejection of what they knew *must* be the truth.

"The problem comes after we are dead because there will be a judgment for us whether we choose to believe in one or not, and then we shall face the only one who can raise us up!"

In the end of the sabbath, as it began to dawn toward the first day of the week, came Mary Magdalene and the other Mary to see the sepulcher. And, behold, there was a great earthquake; for an angel of the Lord descended from heaven, and came and rolled back the stone from the door, and sat upon it. His countenance was like lightning, and his raiment white as snow; and for fear of him the keepers did shake, and became as dead men.

Matthew 28:1-4

The thing that convinces me that the Pharisees knew the truth and rejected it lies in the following verses of Matthew 28:11-15.

Now when they were going, behold, some of the watch came into the city, and showed unto the chief priests all the things that were done. And when they were assembled with the elders, and had taken counsel, they gave (much) money unto the soldiers, saying, Say ye, His disciples came by night, and stole him away while we slept. And if this come to the governor's ears, we will persuade him, and secure you. So they took the money, and did as they were taught; and this saying is commonly reported among the Jews until this day.

These men were not Roman soldiers, but the Pharisees' own temple police guard. "Pilate said unto them, Ye have a watch; go your way, make it as sure as you can."

Who were the deceivers then? Not the Lord Jesus Christ, the Logos of God, or His followers! The deceivers were the Pharisees themselves who knew full well the extent of their deceits!

So let me ask you some questions. Do you remember what Jesus Christ did while He was here on earth? Do you recollect what He said? Do you believe He was who He said He was? Do you remember among those eternal sayings that He claimed He would be raised from the dead three days after His crucifixion? Knowing the proof of His word and the fact that the body disappeared and the Pharisees never did pro-

duce it and display it to put an end to the disciples' witness, let me challenge you to acknowledge His person and ask Him to forgive your rejection of what you have *known* in your heart to be the truth. Ask Him to cleanse you and give you His life, His marvelous resurrec-

THE GARDEN TOMB

tion life! Then you can know that on that great and glorious day, your body will be raised to join your spirit and live forever with Him! For the scripture teaches us "He that hath the Son hath life; and he that hath not the Son of God hath not life" (1 John 5:12).

Eternal life is simply the life of the Eternal One. Don't be a Pharisee remembering the words of "the deceiver" you know is not deceiving. Have the courage of your convictions and become a believer instead of a deceiver of yourself and others!

"*And very early in the morning the first day of the week, they came unto the sepulchre at the rising of the sun. And they said among themselves, Who shall roll us away the stone from the door of the sepulchre? And when they looked, they saw that the stone was rolled away . . .* " (Mark 16:2-4).

"Who Will Roll Away the Stone?"

If you love someone you'll find a way to be with him when all sorts of barriers are placed between. "You'll see me," you whisper when cold fact shouts, "You won't! It's impossible. There's no way." Oh, but love finds a way! I heard about a very strict college that accepted both sexes but imposed rigorous rules upon them. The students were allowed to meet and mix only once a week; on Sundays, walks were allowed—only in opposite directions. The girls were to walk one way and the boys another! What a puzzling thing, therefore, to hear on graduation day varied announcements of engagements! How could this be? Well, love always finds a way!

The women who loved Jesus determined to find a way. Somehow there would be a solution; somewhere there must be an answer to the huge problem that confronted them. As they hurried to the tomb carrying the spices with which to anoint the body of their Lord, they asked each other, "Who will roll the stone away from the entrance of the tomb?" Just *how*, they wondered, was "love" going to deal with *that* one!

Some of us face such a problem this Eastertime. We would love, and we would minister to the loved one, but a great stone lies in the way. Between us and that dear one a great barrier has appeared, one so big that our own puny desires appear ludicrous beside it. Our love seems weak and ineffectual in the face of such an obstacle.

Some of you that read this book say bitterly, "Love can't find a way for me; I know, I've tried." Perhaps you face a hostile teenager and, with your hands full of good things—sweet and special presents carefully prepared—you have hurried toward her only to be confronted with that huge stone of anger or resentment, misunderstanding or deceit. Maybe you have turned to your companions who held in their hands similar gifts for likewise rebellious children and said, somewhat desperately, "Who will roll away the stone for us?"

Let's think about the women in this story. First of all, they loved Jesus. Surely women such as these—Mary Magdalene, Mary the mother of Jesus, and Salome—women who had known and served Christ for years, would have been spared such grief and not been expected to face such a cruel situation. How could God allow these things to happen to those who had served His Son so well? I am often asked this question in modern terms. "Why does God allow me to face such problems when I have been in church, sung in the choir and done no one great wrong? Why must I struggle against such tremendous odds?" We need to take notice of the fact that the women who perhaps knew the Lord Jesus Christ best did not ask "why," they simply asked "who"! They did not even ask "who" had rolled the problem in front of them in the first place. They simply asked, "Who is going to roll it away?"

When faced with problems, one of the tendencies we have is to start dashing around blaming everyone in sight—and even out of sight! "It's God's fault; how come He let it happen to me?" we gripe, especially when we've been in church and given Him all that *money* over the years. Or it's so-and-so's fault; "They've had it in for me for a long time," we say. I always feel sorry for atheists when everything goes wrong for them because they have to find someone to blame, and they can't blame God because they don't believe in Him! They usually end up blaming people. On the other hand, folk who believe in God seem to delight in the fact they have someone to blame. They can get angry at God, the Almighty.

The women in the gospel narrative did not waste valuable moments and useful energy asking *why* God allowed it or *which* wicked soldiers were responsible for their dilemma, they simply asked a very important question, "Just who is going to roll the stone away?" That was not only a sensible attitude to take, it was also a logical question to ask because we are told that the stone was "very great." It was far too big for them to shift on their own, that was obvious; and the disciples were nowhere in sight, so they knew they could not expect any reinforcements. The soldiers could not be relied on to help as they were there to make sure the obstacle stayed firmly in place; in fact, it is doubtful if the women even knew about the soldier guard at all. No, as they hurried toward that insurmountable "mountain" of trouble ahead of them, they couldn't think of anyone in the whole world except Jesus Christ Himself who had the power to roll that stone away; and *that* was their biggest dilemma—Jesus Christ was dead! They had every right to believe He was lying there, sealed into ineffectiveness by the very stone they confronted.

Now when you face an immovable object

in fear, an object that *has* to be moved if love is to have its way, and you know *you* haven't the strength to move it and neither do your friends —however sympathetic they may be—and then, on top of all that sense of inadequacy, when you believe that the God you had trusted in is really unable to help you, you can be forgiven for giving up and running away! But love doesn't give up and love doesn't run away. Love

walks on, even when it believes the object of its love is dead! Love finds something to do even in the face of death. If perfect love had given up or run away, Jesus Christ's body would not have been lying in that tomb in the first place! And what is more important, there could never have been a resurrection.

I remember seeing a poster in a little boy's bedroom. The boy was obviously a great lover

of sports, and his room was festooned with sports "graffiti!" On the wall above his bed hung the intriguing picture of a youngster in football gear sitting on the bench, totally spent, dejectedly musing over his misfortunes. He had obviously "had it" with the game, the coach, and football forever! Underneath, were the two words: "I QUIT." A cross was painted at the side of the poster, and underneath were the succinct words that answered that abdication: "I DIDN'T."

For you see, in giving up, you just *might* be wrong. Wrong, first, about God's ability with stones, soldiers, sepulchers, and things like that! You might not know it, but the God whom you think is dead may just be alive forevermore; and wouldn't it be sad if you turned back before you were shown evidence of that? Some of us only attack a problem if we've figured out all the answers, and that means only the problems that are a safe bet will be tackled!

Where does faith come in if we've figured out all the facts to our liking and are sure of our own strengths and abilities to cope? Faith says, "Face the problem without the answer." Walk right on up to it just as those women did in the gospel story. Take someone with you if you can, for friendship helps keep you from running away. A support group is very necessary in times of crisis; others can help us go on believing in God's intervention when we secretly believe He is dead, too, or inoperative in the situation. C. S. Lewis says, "We talk of Him loudly as being present, but secretly we think of Him as being absent." Someone else's faith will help when our feet falter, and happy is the man who has such friends to turn to in his trouble.

The thing to do in the face of insurmountable problems is walk right on up to them with every intention of walking right on through them if they show no signs of yielding as you approach. If you can't walk through, walk around—find a way past to the Lord, who may or may not move or intervene on your behalf. Somehow we need to live life with the attitude, "I love the Lord; my hands are full of gifts for Him; and one way or the other, I will find Him the other side of the problem." It's certain that

"But go your way, tell his disciples and Peter that he goeth before you . . . " (Mark 16:7).

you'll never arrive at the other side of your problem by running away from it! So face it; face it together with other believers, if possible, and don't blame anyone, for that way you'll exhaust yourself before you ever get there!

I have spent so many years anticipating the stone ahead and practicing rolling it away in my imaginings; I have tried to peer apprehensively around the corner of tomorrow, convinced there are mountains to move just out of sight! "Don't buy what hasn't happened," advised a dear friend of mine as she saw me struggling to move an obstacle that I just *knew* faced me six months in the future. "Why don't you wait until you get there?" she asked. I found out that I could spend all my energy pushing away that stone from "long distance" if I liked, but I would probably end up an emotionally depressed wreck, emptying the moment of confrontation of any resources at all! Don't do that; wait until you get there, will you? Somebody who knows about these things has discovered that eighty percent of the things we worry about never happen anyway! We may as well be using that energy to worry about the stones that *have been* rolled in front of us instead of the ones that *might* or probably *never* will be.

One thing I noticed about these women who went to the tomb was that their love for the Lord Jesus motivated their brave and loving actions even though they couldn't and didn't expect any returns! They knew that He was dead! Facts are facts, but *still* love seeks to do something for the loved one, long after the loved one passes away. Love is eternal, for it lives outside of time. For the love of Jesus, these women insisted on tackling the insurmountable and facing the impossible, even though they believed He was dead!

I remember reading about a believer who was put in prison and tortured for his faith. He was mercilessly brainwashed until he really found himself believing Christianity was in fact a lost cause. His tormentors had managed to transmit into his thought patterns the illusion that Christ had *not* risen from the dead at all, so there was not much point in suffering martyrdom for a dead prophet. What could be the eternal rewards for such illusions? It was obviously sensible to renounce his faith and go free. Sitting in solitary confinement, believing as firmly as these women did in the first century that his God was indeed dead, the man thought the thing through as clearly as he could. He decided that even though Christ was dead, He was still the best man that ever lived and that His way of life outstripped by far any other philosophy around. Yes, the Christian ethic was still worth dying for even though all was lost. He found that in his despair he still loved Christ and would die for the sake of His memory. He would go to his death, not for any heavenly reward, for he did not believe at that point there was one, but because he loved Him. Love does that, lays down its life not expecting any return!

The women hurried on through that early morn toward that huge rock that separated them from the body of their beloved Christ. They were frightened, yes, but they went anyway. Don't wait until you are unafraid before you walk up to the sepulcher. If you can't walk up to it unafraid, walk up to it afraid. And maybe, just maybe, when you get there, you will find "THE STONE HAS BEEN ROLLED AWAY."

In the face of faith and obedience, many a stone has been rolled away, many a sepulcher has been found empty of the dread reality of despair and death, many a soldier has been found laid at our feet. I think of the time I knew I needed to go into the coffee bars of England and tell young people about an alternate philosophy of life. We were youth workers full time with a young people's mission, seeking to reach unchurched teenagers with the Christian gospel. Who shall roll away the stone, I wondered. I was quite convinced no one would let us in to share our message. I couldn't imagine any manager or owner of such places allowing us entrance, but I was wrong. In ten years of such regular outreach ministry, we were *never* once denied entrance. But I would never have known that the stone had been rolled away unless I had asked. When we walked right up to that particular sepulcher, we found the stone had indeed been rolled away. The soldiers we expected to be guarding the precincts were asleep, and we found ample glorious evidence of God's intervention on our behalf!

I remember another time in that youth work when I was asked to speak to hundreds of street kids. We had recruited and organized over thirty churches to try to reach out to the mass of teenagers who were in trouble, who were sleeping on the streets, and who had made their "families" the communes in derelict houses.

There were leather-jacketed gangs and "straight" runaways mixed in with lots of middle-of-the-road kids simply disillusioned with white middle-class answers to their problems. We found ourselves with over a thousand of these youngsters on our hands. Standing on the makeshift platform in a huge warehouse we had scrubbed and polished and decorated for the occasion, my husband sought to speak to that sea of teeming teenage life. He could only manage to be heard for ten minutes at a time, and we used music in between the speeches to give us a chance to mix and meet and "argue" the gospel with them.

At one point my husband told me he wanted me to give the talk the next time around! "Who would roll away that stone?" I wailed. There appeared to me to be a veritable mountain of stones in front of my desired objective! Why yes, I loved the Lord, of course I was willing to bear witness to that, and surely there *was* a service I wanted to render to Him. BUT—the obstacles were enormous! There was the stone of inadequacy; "Who would listen to me?" I wondered. There was the stone of sheer naked fear; "What might they do to me?" Then, there was the stone of disbelief in the power of the things I had to share, "Would the things I said and the way I said them make any definite difference in their lives?" Somehow I managed to walk toward that tomb and climb the step to the platform. And *oh yes*, when I got there, I found the stone had indeed been rolled away. Those whom I expected to oppose me fell silent, just like the soldiers who fell asleep at the tomb; and as I entered into the very place I dreaded entering, anticipating all sorts of deadness, I was met by *life*—for HE IS RISEN indeed!

"Don't be alarmed," the angel assured those

Easter ladies as he sat on the right side of the sepulcher. "You seek Jesus—He is not here—*He is risen*. See the place where they laid Him."

Christ cannot be contained within the tombs of our troubles, inside the sepulchers of our sorrows, or behind the doors of our doubt. No stone can shut Him up nor away from His disciples. The stone still stood there in that quiet garden, a reminder of the reality of the problems we all must live with; but Christ had moved it to one side so very easily, demonstrating His resurrection power on our behalf. So what is the stone you face? As you hurry toward the corner of tomorrow, are you blaming God, the soldiers, the authorities, or the church for your situation? Why not save all that nervous energy for the job He will surely give you—the other side of the stone—that of going and telling His disciples the good, good news of the gospel, "THE STONE IS ROLLED AWAY." "But go," said the angel, "tell His disciples—and Peter!"

"And when they had kindled a fire in the middle of the courtyard and sat down together, Peter sat among them. Then a maid, seeing him as he sat in the light and gazing at him, said, 'This man also was with him.' But he denied it, saying, 'Woman, I do not know him.' And a little later some one else saw him and said, 'You also are one of them.' But Peter said, 'Man, I am not.' And after an interval of about an hour still another insisted, saying, 'Certainly this man also was with him; for he is a Galilean.' But Peter said, 'Man, I do not know what you are saying.' And immediately, while he was still speaking, the cock crowed. And the Lord turned and looked at Peter. And Peter remembered the word of the Lord, how he had said to him, 'Before the cock crows today, you will deny me three times.' And he went out and wept bitterly"

Failure Isn't Final

Have you ever heard the cock crow? I have! There have been many, many times in my life that I, like Peter, have stood tall and straight, looking someone squarely in the eye, and said with honest, sincere earnestness, "I am ready!" I have felt I was adequate for a given situation, gifted for a special task, prepared for a particular assignment; I have known what it was to be eager, excited, dedicated and sure of myself, only to hear the cock crow! I believed I was ready for marriage until the wedding, for motherhood before the baby came, and for church membership before I was given my first responsibility in the fellowship. How can one be so sure about one's capabilities and then fail so miserably? What a dull, sickening realization it is when you discover you were not ready after all and that you've undoubtedly fallen far short of the target.

I suppose failure tastes especially bitter immediately following our most confident assertions. I remember as a young teenager feeling completely sure I was about to beat a tennis opponent in a tournament. "I am ready," I crowed to myself! But something happened to my thirteen-year-old confidence as soon as I stepped onto that lonely court with that sea of eyes set in rows of seemingly critical faces, and I heard the cock crow in no uncertain terms and

lost the most humiliating game of my life!

I have thought of other times, too, that I have crowed to myself or others concerning some clever assessment of my abilities. I well remember one unforgettable occasion when I was sitting on a platform about to speak to an assembly of ladies. I had traveled a long way to give my message. "I am ready, Lord," I intoned in pious yet sincere and earnest prayer. The program began. It continued, and continued, and continued, and quite soon I found myself concluding that it seemed to have no forseeable end in view! I wondered if the motto of the conference was "As it was in the beginning, is now and ever shall be, world without end. Amen!" How could anyone think up so many notices, I wondered? Did we really need to know the whereabouts of the restrooms, what color the doors were and how many? Was it the best use of our time to review the entire program point by point when it was laid out in total clarity in black and white before our very eyes? Then the seminar leaders began to give their previews of the talks they would be giving. They presented them in such detail it seemed superfluous to go to their sessions after they had finished. "I am ready, Lord," I kept reminding Him. "Please hurry them up because they are taking up all my time!" Did I hear a cock crow faintly in the distance?

The Lord Jesus looked right past my voluminous Bible and stack of lecture notes and knew I was no more ready than Simon Peter who had said to Him on that auspicious occasion, "Lord, I am ready to go with thee both to prison and to death." *He* alone could see and hear around the corner of tomorrow! "Before this night is over, Peter," Jesus said to him, "thou shalt deny me thrice!" Before *my* night was over I was to know the humiliating experience of being faced with the fact I was far from ready to deliver my soul of all those clever words assembled in the shape of a sermon. Jesus was about to teach me that my well-prepared soul mattered far more to Him than my well-prepared message! In other words, my attitude was lamentably wrong. I was proud and arrogant and needed reducing to size, which the Lord proceeded to do!

With pride and arrogance, one takes that which rightly belongs to God and applies it to oneself. Pride says I am worth something *apart* from God and acts as Peter, saying in effect, "I am ready to suffer and I expect to do it all on my own; watch me!" After all, Peter knew Jesus wouldn't be able to help him if He was on His way to prison, too! How could He? Peter, confident of his ability to do the right and brave thing, stuck his neck out and fell flat on his face (very painful indeed when your neck is sticking out). That night as I was sitting on that stage in front of all those ladies and saying in effect, "I am worth something apart from God," the Lord decided to teach me a valuable lesson. He was about to show me I was only worth something *because* of Him, not apart from Him at all; and what was more important, my fellow participants were worth a great deal as well! Oh, how I identify with Peter standing proudly in front of Jesus *and* his brother disciples casting a scathing look in their direction and saying with a certain degree of scorn, "Though *ALL* men forsake thee, YET NOT I!" The *all* men he was referring to were very obviously the eleven "others" whom Peter had ceased to respect after having heard Jesus give grave warning of the fact that they would all soon forsake Him. Peter could *very* readily believe the other followers of Jesus could and probably would let Him down, but he could not conceive of the possibility of doing that dreadful thing himself.

The night at that ladies' meeting, the Lord showed me that my proud heart was guilty of a denial as dreadful as Peter's. I was denying the worth of my fellow believers on that program and was trusting not in the Lord, but in the adequacy of my own resources.

"You need to tell these people about your attitude," Jesus said to me as I sat on that stage perched ever so properly in my speaker's chair. "You must ask them for their forgiveness."

"All right, I'll send them a note," I muttered beginning to search around for a piece of paper!

"Oh, no you don't," He said, "tell them."

"How can I tell them?" I asked somewhat desperately as I arranged my features in the right religious look and smiled sweetly at the soloist (who was singing an endless song which appeared to have at least twenty verses).

"Publicly, Peter denied me," He replied, "publicly, he confessed it!"

Suddenly I found myself hoping against hope the soloist would sing at least another twenty stanzas. I thought of the occasion of the meeting on the lakeside after the crucifixion and resurrection of our Lord, and I remembered Peter's conversation with Jesus in front of the same group of men that he had been so quick to dismiss as inferior and weak! That morning, the acrid smell of the charcoal fire must have been a poignant and terrible reminder of another charcoal fire in Pilate's courtyard, and of Peter's abject failure to be the disciple he had believed himself to be! Could it be only such a very few days since he had bragged so dangerously in front of them all, "I'll never, never forsake thee?" "So when they had dined," scripture tells us, "Jesus saith to Simon Peter, 'Simon, son of Jonah, lovest thou me, more than these?' He saith unto him, 'Yea, Lord; thou knowest that I love thee.' He saith unto him, 'Feed my lambs' " (John 21:15).

Failure isn't final, Jesus was saying to Peter; "I still have a task for you to do." But failure must be faced realistically. When Jesus asked Peter if he "loved Him," He used the Greek word *agape* which means to love as God loves. God is primarily concerned with the other's well-being and is prepared to put the other first, regardless of the cost to Himself. *Agape* loves selflessly and is dedicated to a sacrificial giving of itself at all times. When Peter had told his Lord and Savior he would die for Him, he had fully believed he was capable of *agape*. But then the cock crowed, and Peter didn't follow his Lord to prison or to death as he had promised but, instead, followed "afar off," far enough off to avoid the identification with Jesus of Nazareth that might bring him into disgrace or danger. Remembering all of that, Peter answered Jesus' post-resurrection question as to whether he "loved" Him or not with a quiet confession of his failure. "Yea Lord, thou knowest that I 'love' thee," he replied, using the Greek word for human love, *phileo*. *Phileo* means simply to "be fond of" and speaks of the love as between friends. Peter had at last come to terms with himself.

Thinking about those words and Peter's confession, I knew what I needed to do. I needed to tell those dear ladies I had heard the cock crow. I knew that before I could ever get up in front of that waiting assembly and teach the Word of God to others, I had to obey it myself! Do you know how hard that was for me? Here I was, a popular Bible teacher and speaker; how would everyone feel about me if I got up and made such a fool of myself? Who was going to listen to me after that? I may as well not have taken all the effort to come if I were to do such a crazy thing. And surely the Lord didn't want all my precious time and trouble to go to waste! In the end, I did it anyway. Yes, I did it. I did it because I had no alternative. You see, I knew He was giving me another chance. He always does, you know, because failure isn't final! I thanked the Lord I had learned a marvelously valuable lesson and sitting there, bowed my head in prayer and asked Him to make me ready for something I knew I wasn't ready for at all: namely, the opportunity to humble myself, admit my faults, and seek forgiveness from those I'd wronged! I'm sure the ladies thought I was deep in a preparative prayer concerning the message rather than a desperate plea for help concerning the chastened messenger!

It had been necessary for me to learn that an acknowledgment of my own inadequacy was a very necessary ingredient for a servant of His, and I had needed to be forcibly reminded that it would take the adequacy of God to achieve it! When you think you are ready for everything and you discover you are not prepared for anything, that is the start of a new day! But listen to Jesus, hear what He said to Peter! "Feed my sheep, feed my lambs," He said! "Go on, you can now," He was saying to Peter! "Failure isn't final, and now you are ready!" The cock will crow, to be sure, but it will herald the beginning of a new day for us, too, for Jesus never allows a chastened disciple to lie fallow forever. There's too much work to be done!

Rising from my seat at last, I glanced at the clock! To my surprise, the program was running on time. These dear people had not intruded on my portion at all. *It had all been in my mind.* It was a matter of my spirit, that was all, and my impatience with them had merely been a symptom of my arrogance which was having a hard time being upstaged by anyone, however gifted! I sighed; and, leaving my carefully prepared notes on the floor, I turned to the woman sitting expectantly behind me awaiting the address. "Before I can say anything to you, sweet ladies," I started hesitantly addressing the audience, "I have something to say to some other sweet ladies; the ones who have seen fit to invite me to enjoy the privilege of sharing the ministry with them." I turned to each and with the sound of the crowing of that cock ringing in my ears, I said to them, "I'm so sorry; please forgive me for being angry and irritated with you all, for I felt you were taking my time and I want you to know God has soundly rebuked me! I felt I was ready to preach to others but now I know I came onto this platform in my own strength and I recognize I was not ready at all!" They forgave me, of course. *They didn't have my problem!* "*Now* you can feed my sheep," said Jesus, "go on! Hungry sheep are primarily concerned with a good meal; they don't *really* mind who serves it to them. Even failures can lead them to the green pastures!"

So, what do you do when you hear the cock crow? If you are like the rest of us, and like Simon Peter himself, you will begin by crying bitterly! But let me encourage you not to cry forever. Wipe your eyes, for the Lord still hath need of thee! Someone is praying for you all

"... Jesus saith to Simon Peter, Simon, son of Jonah, lovest thou me more than these? He saith unto him, Yea, Lord; thou knowest that I love thee. He saith unto him, Feed my lambs (John 21:15).

this time! Before we ever fail, the God who sees around the corner of tomorrow and knows the whole bitter tragic story has made provision.

He has started praying for you days, months, perhaps even years before you ever deny your Lord. Jesus said, " . . . Simon, Simon, behold, Satan hath desired to have you, that he may sift you as wheat; *BUT I HAVE PRAYED FOR THEE*, that thy faith fail not. And when thou art converted, strengthen thy brethren" (Luke 22:31, 32).

Satan is very uncreative. He hasn't changed his devices one jot since his days in the garden of Eden when he tempted Eve to believe she was ready to do it alone and do without God! Jesus warned Peter that Satan was after him and through Peter he also warned all of us! The devil will laugh all the way back to hell whenever he can get us to puff out our chests and trust in ourselves. It takes Jesus' prayers being answered to make the difference. It always gives me a great thrill whenever I think of Jesus praying for me because I know that's one person who surely has His prayers answered! When I read what He asks for, I am touched beyond measure! He prays that when the testing times come our faith will not fail. What does that mean? Faith means trust. It means leaning hard and heavy upon the Lord, acknowledging our own inadequacy and recognizing our dependence on Him. When my faith fails, or I cease to lean on Him, I start to lean on and trust in me; then I begin to believe I am indeed ready for anything with or without God! So listen, all you failures out there; and hearken, you readers who are identifying with this: after the cock has crowed and you have repented, you will surely hear the Lord giving new orders. Listen to them!

"*When* you are converted (turned around again), strengthen your brethren!" There is work to be done. He will encourage you to share your shortcomings with the people you lead because they will need to know that you are simply an ordinary disciple who is learning to fail successfully, and that failure is *never* final.

"Then Jesus six days before the passover came to Bethany. . . . There they made him a supper; and Martha served. . . . Then took Mary a pound of ointment of spikenard, very costly, and anointed the feet of Jesus, and wiped his feet with her hair: and the house was filled with the odour of the ointment. Then saith one of his disciples, Judas Iscariot . . . Why was not this ointment sold for three hundred pence, and given to the poor? . . . Then said Jesus, Let her alone: against the day of my burying hath she kept this" (John 12:1-7).

The Fragrant Act of Love

Mary loved the Lord Jesus. He had won her heart. She had watched Him at work in the lives of men, women, and children; and sometime, someplace He had opened the door of her life and introduced Himself and she had come to know Him personally. You can know all about someone but have never met him. I have heard all sorts of things about the President of the United States, but I have never met him in person. I feel I know him simply because of the magazines I've read, the TV programs I've watched, the discussions I've had with people, and the information I've gleaned from all sorts of other directions. But there has never come a moment in my life when I have stood with the man face to face, reached out my hand, taken his in mine and said, "Hello, I'm Jill; and you must be the President of the United States!" Many people believe they "know" Christ, but really they only know "about" Him. Perhaps for a long, long time, they have heard stories concerning His deeds—possibly for all of their lives—and maybe they have read books and seen movies about His work, gleaned information—some true and some erroneous—from discussions with others, but never actually had a personal encounter with Him. "But how do you meet Him?" someone may ask. "I can understand how Mary of Bethany could meet

Christ, because Jesus of Nazareth was a real, live human being with a body like hers and an actual flesh and blood hand she could reach out and touch. But He died 2,000 years ago; and even though He was raised from the dead, He ascended into heaven in that human frame that carried Him around this world of ours. So how can *I*, living in the 1980s, meet Him like she did?" Well, the answer to that is you can't meet Him quite the way she did, but we can still meet Him and "know" Him, in another sense.

A body may help us visualize a person, but when I think of human beings I know who live inside their "body houses," I usually think of their personality—their laugh, their sweetness, their character—expressed through that earthly vehicle they inhabit. In other words, the "unseen" part of a person can be known as thoroughly and as completely as the seen. A human body, after all, is merely the means whereby a spiritual entity gets around in a physical environment.

God is three people in one. This is impossible for us to comprehend fully, but the Bible reveals Him to us as such: a trinity comprised of the Father, the Son, and the Holy Spirit. Because we have no similar entity in our experience with which to compare such a being, we find Him difficult to imagine. We can understand the Father because we have or know a father.

*"You can't see the wind, said Jesus, but you can surely
see where it blows and the effect that it has on the
objects it touches! So the Spirit of God cannot be seen
by our physical eyes; but when we invite Him to
'abide' in our hearts, we shall surely 'know' His
presence within us."*

We can understand the Son because we have or know a son. But who has seen a spirit? That is hard to envisage; and because we have no comparison, God the Holy Spirit is dismissed by some people who decide instead to believe not in a trinity but a "binity" comprised of the Father and the Son alone. We cannot, however, simply dismiss the things we do not fully understand. I don't understand electricity but I use it and enjoy it. The trinity has been and is involved in the affairs of men, and we are told in the words of the Westminster Confession that the whole duty of man is to know God and enjoy Him forever!

God the Father worked in creation and on the seventh day rested from all the work that He had made. God the Son accomplished by His death a reconciliation between a holy being who had been offended by our sin and the men and women who would accept His reconciling work on their behalf. Having died, risen again, and ascended into heaven, the risen Christ now sits on the right hand of God. He, too, rests from His work. It is indeed finished.

But man still must be informed about it and be given a chance to apply that reconciling act to his own soul. That is the Holy Spirit's work. It is He who came at Pentecost and, from then to this present day and age, approaches the minds of men, convicting them of sin, convincing them of the rightness of God and the wrongness of many of their deeds, presenting Christ as the object of faith to save them from the certain coming judgment, and regenerating by imparting the forgiveness and very life of God Himself to their souls.

Jesus told Nicodemus that the Holy Spirit is like the wind. Nicodemus was a religious teacher of Israel who still needed to learn these things even though he was a man with a head packed full of knowledge "about" God. You can't see the wind, said Jesus, but you can surely see where it blows and the effect that it has on the objects it touches! So the Spirit of God cannot be seen by our physical eyes; but when we invite Him to "abide" in our hearts, we shall surely "know" His presence within us. There is a compartment in the fabric of the human psyche called the spirit of a man. This is the part within us that makes us different from the animals, that enables us to comprehend spiritual realities, and gives us the power to stop simply running with the pack. It is the part of us that alerts us to the fact that we can know God in the way I have been talking about.

We are made aware of this possibility by a "something missing" feeling. So many people have told me so many times that they are conscious that "something is missing." Not knowing what it is, they wonder if it is a thing, a person, or perhaps a situation or an opportunity they haven't yet encountered or enjoyed. But as things are collected and people added to their lives, and hoped-for situations and opportunities experienced, they become puzzled and distressed because none of that fills up the missing feeling. Someone has aptly said that there's a God-shaped hole inside a person and only God fits into it. When we invite the Holy Spirit to indwell our spirit, a sense of completeness is ours that nothing else and no one else can accomplish in us or for us, and we can say to others, I now "know" Him.

To come to know Christ in this way is an experience many people describe today in various ways. They may say I've been "born again," meaning as they were born once physically, they have now had spiritual life imparted to them and it has been like a "second birth!" They may say that they have been converted, meaning that they have been turned around by receiving the Holy Spirit and by the force of that "wind" within them that has set them off in a totally new direction. They may seek to explain it by saying they have "come to faith," meaning they had "head knowledge" before and now they have "heart knowledge." We need to borrow words and expressions to communicate our experiences, and all of us have varying abilities to make ourselves understood in these matters.

But the question I would ask you is simply this. I would not ask how well you have been able to explain the reality of the experience to someone else, but rather, has there ever come a time in your life when you have had the experience at all? A time when God's unseen Spirit has been invited by you into *your* unseen spirit? Whether you can explain it adequately or not is not the point—what you felt at the time is not relevant either—the important thing is, have you taken that action? You have to open the door of the house in which you live, made of bricks and mortar, for the wind to blow inside; and you need to open the door of your spiritual being, too, in order for the Spirit to enter. "Behold I stand at the door and knock," said the risen Christ in Revelation 3:20. "If any man hears my voice and opens the door I will come in to him and sup with him and him with Me." If you don't know how to invite Him in, stop right now and borrow my words—even as I stopped years ago and borrowed a friend's words—and say:

Lord Jesus, thank you for loving me and dying for me. I realize you had to come and deal with the problem of my sin that has separated me from God. You tell me that on the cross you did indeed deal with it by taking in my place the punishment of God against my wrongdoing. I want to thank you personally for doing that for me. Now by your Holy Spirit, please come into my life. Forgive my sin and turn me around by the sheer force of your personality and help me from this time forth to be inwardly submissive that I may be outwardly obedient. Amen!

If you have just borrowed my words and sincerely meant them, God has heard you and promises you that He has come in. He didn't say He *might* come in; He said He *would*. So when I said at the beginning of this chapter that Mary knew Christ and he "had her heart," this is really what I meant. She had progressed from the position of hearing about Christ to actually knowing Him personally, and He had won her love.

The second thing we can learn about Mary is that Christ did not only own her heart, He enjoyed her home. Paul wrote to some new Christians one day and told them he was praying for them that "Christ would settle down and feel at home" in their hearts. Having come to know Christ through the imparting of Him by the Spirit, He then needed to be made to feel welcome and at home, to sup with them and

they with Him, as Revelation 3:20 puts it. What can this mean to us, and how can we make sure that having accepted Christ into our lives He is glad that He came? Well, let's think for a moment about the reasons Christ must have felt at home in Martha and Mary's house.

We know that He did indeed feel comfortable there because many times we find Him choosing to spend His free time with them. We know also because of the gospel record that tells us Jesus "loved" Martha and Mary and their brother Lazarus. Those three people had become very special friends of His and great supporters of his ministry. Jesus said of Mary "she hath done what she could" and *that* always makes the Lord feel relaxed. Now Mary and Martha and Lazarus were always doing "what they could" for Jesus, and he felt very much at home with them because of it. There was a simple eagerness to serve Him to the limits of their capacity.

Notice the Bible says Mary did what she could; it doesn't say she did what she couldn't! There were things she could do for Christ and there were things she couldn't do. She didn't waste time and energy worrying over the things she couldn't do; she simply made sure she did the things she could. The Lord Jesus never asks more than that. Mary couldn't preach a sermon or sing a solo or write a book, as far as we know; but we do know she could sit at His feet and listen to His word and make that a priority in her life, and we know she helped Martha practically by serving Jesus and His friends at the table and lent a hand making their home available for meetings when the Lord was in town. These were some of the things that she did. She did what she could and Christ felt at home with that.

Once you have invited Christ into your life, you need to begin to do what you can for Him. Don't try to do what others can do. You are you and they are them! You need to say, "Now what could *I* do to serve Jesus that no one else in the whole world could do? What are my gifts and talents, what abilities have I been born with, and what education have I been privileged with, and what gifts do I sense I could exercise on His behalf?" You need to pray that God will show you how you can "do what you can" for Him, and Christ will feel at home with that!

I have found it so exciting to do what I can for Jesus. I have been blessed with a marvelous marriage. We have a home, so I've done what I could and made it available for people and for meetings. It has been a place to run to for rebellious teenagers and confused adults. I've been able to cook meals and feed and serve them so these damaged people could relax and meet Jesus there. I've been able to take my teacher training and do what I could for Jesus with it—teaching in Sunday School, in church, and in homes. I've been able to pick up a pen and write about God, and I've been able to produce plays and dramas concerning His life and His doings. These are some of the things *I've* been able to do. I've done what I could, and I have come to realize this makes Him feel very much at home in my life! Let me ask you, what are some of the things *you've* been able to do? Have you done what *you* could?

But Christ not only had Mary's heart and her home, He had Mary's hidden treasure, too! I'm speaking of the box of ointment. The Bible tells us it was "very precious." That little alabaster box of spiknard was not a possession to be parted with lightly, and Christ did not demand it of her. Knowing all things, He knew it had not been given; but he did not ask for it, he did not demand it of her. No, Mary knew she was quite free to keep her hidden treasure hidden. Her little box of very precious ointment may have been her marriage box, security for her in case she never married, an investment for her future. She didn't need to give it up. She didn't need to pour it out in a display of loving joy; but she did anyway, anointing the head and feet of Jesus Christ. She did this, the Bible implies, because she only, of all the Lord's disciples, understood His repeated statements about His approaching crucifixion, and she wanted to do what she could and anoint His body beforehand, for burial. Overcome with the fact that her beloved Lord was about to die for her, she brought the most precious treasure she had and in loving response gave it in such a manner it was impossible ever to retrieve. We are told "the aroma of the ointment filled the house" that day and that fragrant act of love became an eternal action that would make Mary an example to all men in all ages! "Verily I say unto you," said Jesus, "Wheresoever this gospel shall be preached . . . this also that she hath done shall be spoken of for a memorial of her" (Mark 14:9).

I believe that many of us can know Christ and love Him, and that many of us can have given Him our hearts and even our homes, can

"*Christ not only had my heart, but He had my home as well . . . But there was a hidden little box that no one knew about that had not been given.*"

have sat at His feet and listened to His word, but that few among us bring our hidden treasures, our little boxes, and pour them out for Christ. The reasons we do not are varied. Perhaps we are prevented by the criticism of the disciples or the snide remarks of his enemies. "Don't go overboard," we hear people say. "Have enough religion to make you respectable but don't go in for this born again thing." "It's not necessary," others say. "You can waste your life and miss out on the best things by getting involved in such excesses of Christianity." What do you, and what do I know of Mary's sacrifice? *What fragrance of abandonment permeates the atmosphere of my personality in such a way that those who watch my actions will never forget the eternal worth of them?*

I remember God speaking most forceably to me from this passage of Scripture. I was a young missionary, struggling with a problem. Christ had my heart. I had met Him personally some years previously and had been "doing what I could" for Him ever since. That willingness to serve had led me into full-time involvement with my husband in a youth organization working among teenagers. Christ not only had my heart, but He had my home as well. Small though our little house was, it was always full of all sorts and conditions of people. In fact my mother once said to me with a chuckle, "Jill your house is just like Piccadilly Circus!" But there was a hidden little box that no one knew about that had not been given. Mine, like Mary's, was very precious. It happened to be my marriage. My husband had been called away from home for months on end to establish other youth centers around the world and to train and encourage those who ran them. How hard I worked at giving that little box to Christ. But I discovered I was not the "Mary" missionary I had imagined myself to be. I couldn't, or I should say wouldn't, give that little box to Him. How could I possibly find the strength to give my marriage to God?

There came a time, however, when sick with the struggle I knelt in prayer and told Him all about my battle and how I had learned some things about myself that I had not enjoyed discovering at all. I had found out I would never be able to be a Mary and break that box myself, but I gave Him leave to take it anyway. I asked Him to help me by walking into that closed room in my life and by breaking the box for me. He did; and the fragrance must have filled the house, for from that moment of commitment, people began to sense an aroma that attracted them to the Christ that lived within me. Our marriage was touched with a sweetness never enjoyed before and even though a few disciples said such things as "What a waste. Why does Stuart travel so much and Jill stay home? Why if they were together this marriage could *really* be used by God!" We knew, Stuart and I, that nothing mattered but the fact that the box was broken, the marriage given, and, together, we were freer than we'd ever been before—to do what we could for Him! So my friend, whoever you are out there, is there a little box, a hidden treasure in the attic of your life that no one else knows about save Jesus? Maybe it is like mine, a marriage box, or perhaps it is one of another sort. Identify it, if you can. Name it upon your knees before God. Can you, or rather *will* you give Him permission to take it? If you do, I can tell you with surety that from that time on there will be a perfume about your service and a touch about your life that will suggest to others a fragrant sense of Him!

Indwelt

Not only by the words you say, not only in your
    deeds confessed,
But in the most unconscious way is Christ
    expressed.
Is it a beautific smile, a holy light upon your
    brow?
Oh, no! I felt His presence when you laughed
    just now.
For me, 'twas not the truth you taught, to you
    so clear, to me so dim,
But when you came to me, you brought a sense
    of Him.
And from your eyes He beckons me and from
    your lips His love is shed,
Till I lose sight of you and see the Christ
    instead.

Beatrice Cleland

"How then shall they call on him in whom they have not believed? And how shall they believe in him of whom they have not heard? And how shall they hear without a preacher?" (Rom. 10:14).

Start Where You Are

Luke, the beloved physician and companion of the apostle Paul, was one of the first historians of the early church. He wrote an orderly and historically correct account of the life of the Lord Jesus Christ in two parts. The first part is called the Gospel of Luke; the second is the Acts of the Apostles, although some have suggested it should rather have been called the Acts of the Holy Spirit. This book continues the post-resurrection story of the life of the Lord Jesus lived out through the bodies of ordinary men and women. Luke tells the man to whom he is writing, whose name is Theophilus, that his gospel is a record of all Jesus *began* both to do and teach until the day "He was taken up," that is, the day of the ascension. The Book of Acts, then, is a continued orderly account of the works of the risen Chist manifested through believers—made visible through changed men! Let us take a closer look at some of those tranformed people.

The disciples were certainly going to have to be different if they were to fulfill Christ's mandate. Sometime during those forty days of His post-resurrection ministry, Jesus had told them, "Ye shall be witnesses unto me." Just who was He talking to? He was addressing eleven men who had failed dismally to be witnesses to anything other than their own cowardice. How were such men going to be able to bear the weight of the responsibility to go into all the world and preach the gospel to every creature? Take Peter, for example. Standing in Pilate's courtyard warming himself at the charcoal fire, surrounded by curious palace personnel, he had had a marvelous opportunity to be a witness for Jesus. At that particular time there were, alas, only witnesses against Him. As Jesus was being interrogated and Peter stood near at hand shivering nervously, a little maid took a closer look into the face of the big fisherman and challenged him to state his allegiance.

"Then said the maid that kept the door, unto Peter, art not thou also one of this man's disciples? He saith, I am not" (John 18:17). How would Peter, frightened into silence by a little maid, ever be brave enough to confess Christ before men? As he waited miserably, acutely aware of the soldiers' scrutiny, one of the servants of the high priest who was a kinsman to the man whose ear Peter had cut off, suddenly asked him the crucial question: "Did not I see thee in the garden with Him?" Peter, we are told, quite understandably denied it again! (John 18:26, 27). Can you imagine Peter, who in the past had been terrified of a servant of the high priest, becoming bold enough to care little for the repercussions of his witness in the future? It was obviously going to take a big change in the man for him to behave differently.

Jesus, knowing all things, had already planned on Pentecost making the difference, and that's why we find Him telling the disciples to wait for the promise of the Father (the giving of the Holy Spirit) which He had already spoken to them about. He told them to wait in Jerusalem for that which He had promised which would occur "not many days hence" (Acts 1:5).

Read Peter's sermon on the day of Pentecost (Acts 2:14-36), and you will wonder if you are reading about the same men. What a fantastic change the imparting of the Holy Spirit made in all the disciples' lives and particularly in Peter's ministry. Read the events in the Book of Acts and you will find the man who had been frightened of a little girl and threatened by a servant of the high priest, standing up unashamed and unafraid in front of literally hundreds of relatives of the Pharisees (and no doubt many little maids), not to mention the crowds of strangers and foreigners who had traveled to Jerusalem for the feast of Pentecost. Just listen to him informing the whole house of Israel in no uncertain terms that "God hath made that same Jesus, WHOM YE HAVE CRUCIFIED, both Lord and Christ" (Acts 3:36). It took the Holy Spirit to change a sniveling coward into a courageous courier of the good news about Jesus!

As ordinary men and women heard the message through the lips of the transformed apostles, many believed, turned to the Lord and received the gift of the Spirit for themselves. Then the persecution of Stephen arose and scattered those early believers abroad. They fled, gossiping the gospel about them as they went. If we are to be witnesses to Him in the day and age in which we live, we shall not be able to do it without the enabling of the Holy Spirit. We need our own personal Pentecost that will change us from retreating rabbits into roving lions for Him!

Having thought about the men, let us think next about the mandate. "Go ye into all the world," said Jesus, and as you go "preach the gospel to every creature" (Mark 16:15)"... and,

lo, I am with you alway, even unto the end of the world!" (Matt. 28:20b).

Jesus never does things by halves and He didn't intend for us to either. He wanted His followers to know He would make them whole men that they might take His whole message to the whole world. The disciples were not to confine their evangelism to Jerusalem but to start there, spreading the word in ever increasing circles. We must have a vision of the whole world if we are to be true to the mandate we have been given. John Donne said that "no man is an island"; and now, as we find ourselves in this "global village" there is no longer an excuse for the believer to be uniformed about the needs of the world, or to be unable to go around the entire circumference of it by one means or another.

First of all, we need to pray about taking the good news ourselves. Try praying, "Lord, would You have me to stay?" rather than "Lord, would You have me to go?" Examine your heart and see if you are indeed willing; and if you find in all honesty you are not, then pray thus, "Lord, I am willing to be made willing." Surround yourself with information concerning opportunities to serve overseas. Read much about the third world countries, or the need in Europe or anywhere else you think He might call you to be. If you cannot go yourself, contribute to a missionary agency and go with your money instead; and (last, but not least) make sure you regularly go in your prayer life!

Yes, go somehow, someway into all the world. "But what do I say if I do go?" you may ask. "What words would I use, for I do not see myself as a great orator!" You don't need to be a great orator to tell what you know, and Jesus has never expected us to tell what we don't know! The man born blind from birth (as related in the ninth chapter of John), having been healed by Christ, was asked by the Pharisees just who had made him whole? They wanted to know who had made the difference in his life. The man knew nothing of theology or of Jesus of Nazareth, but he did his best and told what he knew, which was precious little. "Once I was blind and now I see," he simply said to his interrogators! As the questions grew more in-

"But ye shall receive power, after the Holy Ghost is come upon you; and ye shall be witnesses unto me both in Jerusalem, and in all Judaea, and in Samaria, and unto the uttermost parts of the earth" (Acts 1:8).

tense, the boldness of the man increased and he ended up giving the belligerent Pharisees a run for their money! Here was a very ordinary man who had been touched and transformed by God's power, telling *his* world all about it. He certainly didn't get any marks for converts; but after he had been summarily dumped by his audience, he discovered himself found by the Son of God and grew immeasurably in his knowledge of the Lord. I haven't a doubt in my mind that, having done so well with his first sermon, he was now ready and armed to do better with his second!

There is something extremely motivating about sharing your faith. It drives you to know Christ and to understand His Word in order to answer the questions you are asked. When I was working with a youth organization in Europe, we took church-going youngsters onto the streets for open-air services. I watched "church mice" turned into "mighty men" before my very eyes! The challenge of defending their belief was the motivating force behind that change. As we returned to the safety of our church precincts, they demanded all sorts of Bible study from their leaders to better equip themselves for the fray. Having been thrown into a situation where they had to declare themselves *for* Christ and say in effect "Once I was blind, but now I can see," they were no longer content to keep their minds in neutral concerning their faith. What was more, as soon as some of those unreached teens turned to the Lord, through the young believers' witness, our "learner" evangelists discovered it was not enough to go out hunting for spiritual scalps, but rather they needed to make disciples, teaching them to observe all things whatsoever He had commanded.

So to go into all the world is the first thing; but having gone, the second thing we must do is make sure we tell all the people ALL THE GOSPEL. This will mean we explain the three tenses of salvation. The word *saved* is used in three different ways in the Bible. It is used in the past, present, and future sense; so it is possible to know I have been saved from the *penalty* of sin, but it can also be a glorious reality to experience a "saving" in the present

from the *power* of my sin, and in the eternal future I can be fully assured I shall be saved from the very presence of my sin! There is much more to being a Christian than merely becoming one, just as there is more involved in being a human being than simply being born. The *all* of the gospel we need to tell to *all* of the world is how that continuous saving experience can be realized in our lives. Becoming a Christian can happen in a moment, but being the Christian we have become is another matter. That requires *discipline*, which is the very word from which *disciple* is derived.

Many people in America have been born again but have never been taught what to do next. "Is that all there is to it?" a girl asked me after walking to the front of a church in response to a gospel invitation. What she was asking in effect was, "Is that the end of it?" I was able to tell her, "No, that's not the end of it, *that's the beginning of it!*" Our relationship with our living Lord can be likened to a marriage. We can begin it with an event of religious significance, when both parties make a pledge to love and honor; but the idea is then to spend a lifetime getting to know, understand, and enjoy each other. My husband, who is in the business of hatching, matching, and dispatching, in other words, the pastorate, often tells young couples that a wedding lasts a day but a marriage is forever, and to be careful not to confuse the two! The good news we have to share is that Christ, our spiritual bridegroom, invites His bride—the church, made up not of bricks and mortar but of living stones, namely individuals —not only to a wedding, but to a marriage! That ongoing relationship that now needs nurturing is part and parcel of the *whole* gospel.

So the mandate the disciples received was to go into *all* the world and preach all the gospel to all the people. "To *all* the people," means we are not to be selective and tell only the folk we like, but to share the news with those we don't much care for as well. We are not to choose our audience but rather be content for Him to choose it for us. We are to tell the bright and the slow, the old and the young, the black and the white, the rich and the poor. This means we are going to have to move outside our church

buildings and reach the people who don't make a habit of worshiping. What's the point of telling only those who have already heard it all. Most of us have the idea that church is the place we should preach to people and there it should stay. But that's like fishing in a swimming pool. We have to go to the muddy streams and rivers outside our ecclesiastical boundaries to fish for the "big ones" who have not yet been "caught" instead of wasting our time and energy telling the ones who *have* already been caught that they need to be caught again! Church should be the place where we instruct the caught how to catch others, as well as a place we can bring the newly netted to be nurtured and fed! Jesus said, "*Go into all the world to every creature.*" He didn't say, sit in church pews and expect them to come to you! "Every creature" will not be found attending church, not in this day and age. You will find some of

"It seemed the Lord was telling me to start at
Jerusalem and the impact of my obedience would
ripple out, and out, and out until I would indeed find
myself touching the whole, wide world."

them in your office and some in your clubs, some in the supermarket and some on the planes, some on the tennis courts and some in the bowling alleys. Each one has a right to hear the good news.

"But just where do I start?" you may wonder. Perhaps you feel you are just an ordinary person living in an extremely mundane situation. If you have understood you can begin to bank on an extraordinary God inside of you who will enable you, as he enabled Peter, to speak boldly (whereas before you were too frightened to even try), then you are indeed ready to learn about the method of witnessing. Acts 1:8 tells us just what that method is. We are to begin at Jerusalem. That means, just where we are. The only way every man is going to be reached is when every Christian starts in his own Jerusalem. We are to start where we are with what we have! The mission field is between our own two feet. Take note then: every person is either a missionary or a mission-field.

I remember living in the heart of the country in a small cottage. I was surrounded by little old ladies living in similar little cottages. I can remember a period in my life when I became pretty frustrated because I had a great vision for the whole world and I wanted to tell every man in it about my Lord. But I had three small children at the time and a husband who traveled a great deal, so I needed to stay home and attend to my responsibilities. I remember leaning over a little bridge and dropping a pebble into the still pool beneath. As it fell into the middle of the pool and the ripples of its impact moved out and out until they touched the very outer edges of that water, I was reminded of Acts 1:8: "But ye shall receive power, after that the Holy Spirit is come upon you: and ye shall be witnesses unto me both in Jerusalem, and in all Judaea, and in Samaria and unto the uttermost part of the earth." It seemed the Lord was telling me to start at Jerusalem and the impact of my obedience would ripple out, and out, and out until I would indeed find myself touching the whole, wide world. How could that possibly be, I wondered?

But I began to do as I was told and take the whole gospel to my whole world just where I was—in my Jerusalem. I went around my neighborhood and knocked on all the doors of those little, old ladies; and after many weeks of patient perseverance, ten or eleven were coming to our small home. Within a year or two the ripple had widened to "Judaea," and we began a youth work that spread to the surrounding villages. Through the children that we met, an outreach operation was instigated in "Samaria" among the despised youngsters that no one else would touch—the gangs and the lost drug children of the 60s—just as in Jesus' day no one would touch the despised Samaritans and lepers. The ripple rippled on and out as people from other countries with children in like difficulties heard about the success of our "method" and wrote to us asking that we might come and teach them how to do it. When we wouldn't come, they asked us to write books or articles, explain it in letters, and make tapes, until today, twenty years later, the ripples have and are indeed touching the uttermost parts of the earth!

But you have to start where you are with what you've got! If everyone who has been reached would only do that, then the whole world would soon be reached! This, I believe, is the method we must use! I am not saying we do not need to use other methods also, such as the media or all the modern technological helps we have to bring the whole gospel to the whole world. We need to remember, however, that these things are only tools; the greatest instrument that every child of God has at his disposal is the Spirit of the living God whose work it is to change a man who, in turn, changes other men.

So we have talked about the men and we have spoken of the mandate, discussed the message and contemplated the method, remembering that it all started on that grand resurrection day! The Acts of the Apostles, then, is not merely a book of the Bible placed snugly between the Gospel of John and the first Chapter of Corinthians, but a gloriously exciting account of the Acts of the Holy Spirit begun at Pentecost and continued even now in the lives of ordinary people like you and like me!

"And beginning at Moses and all the prophets, He expounded unto them, in all the scriptures the things concerning Himself" (Luke 24:27).

The Things Concerning Himself

One thing that is a sheer delight to me is the time I daily spend with the risen Lord Jesus Christ. It is then that He shares with me from His word "The things concerning Himself."

The following thoughts are some of my own personal blessings from these happy times with Him. I have included thoughts for ten days to use, if you wish, to start a regular time with God. These short devotionals include a verse to read, something to think about, and a subject to pray about. Soon you will be able to write down your own thoughts. Here are some hints to help you begin.

1. Set aside 15 minutes a day, preferably at the same time.
2. Find a quiet place where you can be alone.
3. Read 10 verses of the scriptures. If you don't know where to begin, try Philippians.
4. Underline the promises in green, the warnings in blue, and the verse you like best in red.
5. Keep a notebook and write out the verse you like best.
6. Write a paragraph about the verse, saying why you like it.
7. Pray about what you have written.

After a few months, you will need to buy a bigger notebook!

Day 1

Trusting

"The Lord is my strength and my shield; my heart trusted in Him, and I am helped: therefore my heart greatly rejoiced; and with my song will I praise Him" (Ps. 28:7).

I had a burden; someone I loved needed shielding. I asked Jesus to tell the Father and, of course, He did. The Father told Jesus to tell me He'd look after it for me. Jesus told me. The next day I was driving along the highway in my car. I asked Jesus to remind the Father about my burden. He told me THE FATHER WOULD LIKE TO REMIND YOU HE DIDN'T NEED REMINDING! I was the one who needed that! I needed to be reminded my burden was being cared for. The next day I knelt in prayer. I told Jesus to tell the Father I loved Him. Jesus told the Father. The Father told Jesus to thank me and tell me He would like to hear me say something else. He would like to hear me say, "And I trust You, too!"

Think about trusting Him. List some of the blessings of the trusting heart that you find in the following verses: Psalm 32:10, Psalm 37:3, Psalm 125:1. Tell Him you trust Him.

Day 2

On Being Too Spiritual with Your Husband

My waking thought was of my husband Stuart's fine sermon on Noah and his ark. Earnestly looking into what I could see of Stuart's 6:00 A.M. eyes, I said intensely, "Darling, I want to be like Mrs. Noah today! You are my Noah and I think of you, providing and building an ark so you can invite people to come in out of the judgment of God! I want to be your helpmeet in this wonderful work."

There was silence and then, "Good. Why don't you get up then, and clean the ark?"

We can be far too spiritual, especially at 6:00 A.M. or at 12:00 P.M. Our husbands see us furiously studying 1 Corinthians 13, surrounded by books, concordances, and tomes of explanation instead of feeling our arms around them in a demonstration of the very love we are academically exploring. The animals need feeding, Mrs. Noah! Let's be up and at 'em!

Let us pray our love will be eminently practical.

Day 3

Favorite Child

"This is my beloved Son, in whom I am well pleased. . . . Who his own self bare our sins in his own body on the tree. . . " (Matt. 3:17; 1 Pet. 2:24a].

"I want to be Your favorite child, Father!"
"You do?"
"Yes, I really do; that sounds like fun!"
"My favorite child like who?"
"Well, like Jesus."

"Then flatten out your hands upon My cross,
Pile foot on foot that nails may stave them in.
Hang high, hang long above the blood-soaked turf
And bear my judgment deep upon your soul for others' sin
Then, go to hell, my child,
    My favorite child!"

"Oh! That doesn't sound like much fun after all!"

Pray about the costly "privileges" of being a "favored" son of God.

Day 4

On Prayer for a Coveted Position

". . . not my will, but thine, be done" (Luke 22:42b).

"I'm going away Pete," I informed our youngest son. "I'll pray about the selections of players for your basketball team, that the right thing will happen for you."

Pete shot me a somewhat apprehensive glance, then. "Don't do that, Mom," he pleaded. "Just pray I make the team!"

Teenage sentiments? Amusing? But, O Lord Jesus Christ, how like my praying! So often, I don't *want* the right thing to happen, I just want to make the team.

Teach me to pray and mean, "Not my will, but Thine be done."

Which place on which team? Remember only to play for Him.

"Help me to spend time asking God for the dimensions of the structure we must build for the blessings of our family."

Day 5

God Shut the Door

"Come thou and all thy house into the ark . . . and the Lord shut him in" (Gen. 7:1, 16).

Noah was building something he'd never built before. It was going to shield his family. So we must build. We should always be listening for God's instructions so we can be creating something new in our relationships with our loved ones that they may be blessed. But you say, "We tried everything I know and there is still hostility, misunderstanding, and estrangement." Just as God instructed Noah with the specifics of the ark, we must ask Him for the dimensions of a new structure so we will be forced to spend more time in close contact with our family. He gives the ideas.

We mustn't shut out the people who should be close to us but let God shut them in to us. Then one day, when we have spent our "40 days" locked up together, we will find the door opened to new heights. The ark rested on Mount Ararat, which was almost a heavenly situation and one which became a new world of discovery for Noah's family.

Help me to spend time asking God for the dimensions of the structure we must build for the blessings of our family.

Day 6

God Shut the Lions' Mouths

Now when Daniel knew that the writing was signed, he went into his house; and his windows being open in his chamber toward Jerusalem, he kneeled upon his knees three times a day, and prayed, and gave thanks before his God, as he did aforetime.

Daniel 6:10

Why did Daniel find himself in the den of lions? Because he prayed three times a day!

Have you noticed that the worst things happen to the best people? We unconsciously believe that God will save us from the den of lions if we are a good little boy or girl and say our prayers regularly! Then we are hurt when He doesn't.

What did God *do* for Daniel because of his relationship with Him? He shut the lions' mouths!

God didn't save Daniel *from* the situation; He saved him *in* it.

Pray about some of the worst things that are happening to the best people you know. Pray for a "den deliverance" for them.

Day 7

Catalogs

". . . and the Lord . . . let none of his words fall to the ground" (1 Sam. 3:19a).

I love ordering things from catalogs. The specifics are like a hard crossword puzzle with all the answers provided, making you feel really grand—clever and all that—because you can fill them in!

The request is posted and forgotten in the rush of more immediate things. Then, right in the middle of something totally unrelated to the catalog order, the delivery man delivers!

How like God. The specifics of my order are carefully tabulated and delivered in His time and with eternal efficiency. Prayers I prayed months, even years ago, are delivered faithfully long after the need is forgotten. He could forget; I think sometimes it wouldn't really matter, but my words are not allowed to fall to the ground. Angels catch them and register the demand. How good of God.

Sometimes, however, the goods don't look quite the same as the ones I ordered, but there is a difference with our heavenly requests. The goods that finally arrive will be found to fit perfectly.

Spend some moments thinking and thanking Him for prayers prayed but forgotten that He has faithfully remembered and answered.

Day 8

A Den of Prayer

"My God hath sent His angel, and hath shut the lions' mouths, that they have not hurt me" (Dan. 6:22).

We were enjoying a prayer meeting. That's right, enjoying, not enduring! Fifteen ladies were meeting to talk to God. To encourage our hearts, we were reading together from His Word, and we marveled at Daniel, noting that something wonderful happened everytime he prayed.

"How brave and courageous he was," sighed one.

"How close he kept to the Father," said another.

"How special his gifts and how faithful a servant," said a third.

There was silence.

"What I like best about this story," said my friend, "concerns the lions. If God shut the lions' mouths, I know He can surely shut mine." We prayed about that, all of us.

Day 9

He Knows Something
We Don't Know

"I am . . . the first and the last" (Rev. 1:11a).

How good of God to shield the future from us. How could we live well or sleep easily if we but knew the death we'd die, the child who would go wrong, the house that would burn to the ground, or the poverty we might endure? For us, our language must be full of words like "maybe," "perhaps," or "someday." But He knows something we don't know. His language consists of the *shall be* and *will be* because He knows ahead, whereas we but know behind.

Then to know Him who knows the "something I don't know" is comfort indeed. For, knowing all, He waits ahead for us, surprising us with steady provisions of His love.

Praise Him for the things He "has been," as the "first" and for the things He "will be" as the last. And remember, He knows something we don't know.

Day 10

The Prodigal Prig

". . . am I my brother's keeper? . . . For this my son, was dead, and is alive again" (Gen. 4:9b; Luke 15:24a).

There's a prig in the pew
  And a son in the stew.
    What's new?

Either pigsty or pew,
  The view is the same,
    it stinks.

Son number one goes home,
  Dirtier but wiser for his dine
    among the swine.

Son number two is home already
  but wishes he wasn't!
    I don't like this chap;
      He doesn't like his dad;
        He's mad and sad;
          He feels he's been had.

Wallowing in his pigsty of prejudice,
  he mourns the fatted calf.
    Why kill the cow? Now?
    Why not then? When?
Oh, for my friends, prejudiced prigs,
  pious, pompous, pitiable,
    play actors like me;
      not for my brother who blew it!

It is sometimes hard to love and care for our brothers and sisters. Be honest, be sorry, then be different! Pray for them.

That Calvary Be Worthwhile

Lord, where can we go but to Thee?
We have no one in heaven beside Thee,
and no one on earth with your grand ability
to touch our spirits,
lift our mood,
bless our kids,
stick us back together again when we fall apart
or sew a torn relationship into place.

We come to ask for the consciousness
of your immediate and dynamic presence,
that your messengers be greatly helped
and that you would have mercy upon us, O God.

We wonder what you see that we cannot:
A crowd of cowards?
A sea of sin?
A morass of people picking and clawing at each other?
Hurt husbands or rejected wives
who find it difficult to look their neighbors in the face?
Or do you, perhaps, see those of us who are celebrating:
the "I have need of nothing" individuals,
the "keep your religion, I have mine" group,
The cynic or the scoffer,
or even little children capable of huge injustice
on their own sweet level.

See, Lord, we are here together;
have mercy on us all.
Find us tonight, God, find us.
Nudge us into your will and away from our wants;
reduce us to size,
show us your mighty arm;
carry away our sin.
O Lord, be yourself;

Move us into action, a bold stand,
a walking statement that will tell the world,
our world, that Jesus is our public choice.

We ask for the awareness that something is going on;
we request that you fasten our minds with the
nail of urgency to the wall of decision;
and we ask it all, Jesus,
that Calvary be worthwhile.
Amen.

Jill Briscoe
Prayer at the Billy Graham
Greater Milwaukee Crusade, 1979